People, Parks, and Perceptions

A History and Appreciation
of Indiana State Parks

Glory-June Greiff

Woodsprite Press   *Trafford Publishing*   *2009*

Order this book online at www.trafford.com
or email orders@trafford.com

Most Trafford titles are also available at major online book retailers.

Note for Librarians: A cataloguing record for this book is available from Library
and Archives Canada at www.collectionscanada.ca/amicus/index-e.html

Printed in Victoria, BC, Canada.

ISBN: 978-1-4269-0369-4 (sc)
ISBN: 978-1-4269-0371-7 (e)

Trafford rev. 6/9/2009

 www.trafford.com

North America & international
toll-free: 1 888 232 4444 (USA & Canada)
phone: 250 383 6864 ♦ fax: 250 383 6804 ♦ email: info@trafford.com

The United Kingdom & Europe
phone: +44 (0)1865 487 395 ♦ local rate: 0845 230 9601
facsimile: +44 (0)1865 481 507 ♦ email: info.uk@trafford.com

Dedicated to the memory of
my mother, June Fritz Greiff
1921-2008
and
my father, William R. Greiff
1919-1981
who instilled in me a lifelong love of woods and waters.

People, Parks, and Perceptions
A History and Appreciation of Indiana's State Parks

CONTENTS

ACKNOWLEDGMENTS

One cannot begin to write acknowledgments without a sense of trepidation. It would be impossible to name all those to whom I owe a debt of gratitude for the help they gave toward the completion of this work. If I have inadvertently left anyone unmentioned, I do most humbly apologize.

Some parts of this book evolved from my master's thesis, "Parks for the People: New Deal Work Projects in Indiana State Parks," completed in 1992, and also benefited from research undertaken for a discrete survey and a multiple property nomination of New Deal resources in Indiana state parks, under the auspices of the Indiana Division of Historic Preservation and Archaeology, in 1990-1991. Much of this research was carried out in the National Archives in Washington, D.C. and the Franklin D. Roosevelt Library in Hyde Park, New York; in both institutions several of the staff were especially helpful and kind.

Ruth Barker at the University Library at IUPUI doggedly searched for obscure government publications of the 1920s and 1930s through interlibrary loan, always managing to find repositories that did not charge fees, important to a struggling graduate student. Then and later, the staff at the Indiana State Library were especially helpful in unearthing additional related material to that which I requested; special thanks to David Lewis, Barney Thompson, Darrol Pierson, and Martha Wright.

My work could not have been completed without extensive field studies in the Indiana State Parks, and infinite thanks are due to the park naturalists, assistant managers, and managers who assisted me in so many ways. In recognition of their extra efforts I must single out Jim Eagleman, Dick Davis, and Fred Wooley, longtime naturalists (now *interpretive* naturalists, thank you!) at Brown County, Clifty Falls, and Pokagon, respectively.

Likewise I must thank the several DNR and parks administrators, past and present, who allowed me to interview them at length for their insights. I am particularly grateful to Gerald J. Pagac, former Director of the Division of State Parks and Reservoirs, for his patience and willingness to respond to what must have seemed a never-ending barrage of questions over time. His successor, Daniel W. Bortner, was very helpful as well.

Scores of CCC veterans and former WPA workers recounted their experiences to me; I am especially grateful for the invaluable help and indomitable enthusiasm of the late Roger Woodcock, who once split rocks and plied a masonry trowel at Pokagon. I have been honored to attend the reunion of CCC Company 556 every year at that park since 1991.

A number of people have aided the project by reading all or parts of the manuscript in its various incarnations, starting with the thesis, for which my committee of Dr. Patrick J. Furlong, the late Dr. Scott J. Seregny, and Dr. Ralph D. Gray were all helpful in a variety of ways. Dr. Gray also read later chapters of the manuscript. I have not forgotten Dr. Philip J. Scarpino, who constantly challenged me during the writing of the thesis, and urged me onward as I expanded the project to explore the history of another seventy-five years beyond the New Deal. Phil read and critiqued an earlier draft of this work, to its betterment. Thanks, too, to Dr. Rebecca Conard and Dr. Susan L. Flader, authors, respectively, of state parks histories in Iowa and Missouri, each of whom read the second draft and offered useful suggestions that I took to heart. And thanks to outside readers Joseph Cunningham and Eric Grayson. William Gulde, former head of Social Studies at North Central High School in Indianapolis, read through the penultimate draft and offered valuable perspectives at the eleventh hour.

Eric Grayson was also especially helpful in areas of technical expertise, translating my second draft out of hopelessly outdated computer technology into something that, while still outdated (Luddite that I am in these matters), I could use and others were able to read. Thanks, too, are due Eric for his technical help on scanning and digitizing old photographs, translating a later draft into a still newer format, and helping to design the layout. Al Zimmerman scanned my Kodachrome slides, which Eric also digitized. Thanks to Greg Dunn for the author's photo.

Part of the initial research for this book was funded through a Clio Grant from the Indiana Historical Society. I am eternally grateful to the late Robert M. Taylor, Jr., who unfailingly supported this project. Later research and writing was funded in part by a grant from the United States Department of the Interior, National Park Service Historic Preservation Fund, administered by the Indiana Department of Natural Resources, Division of Historic Preservation and Archaeology. The content and opinions do not necessarily reflect the views or policies of the Department of the Interior or the Indiana Department of Natural Resources. For their faith in and willingness to support the publication of this book, I am grateful to Jon C. Smith (now with the National Park Service) and Steven D. Kennedy.

Many thanks to J. Scott Keller for financial support toward the preparation of he manuscript, given in memory of Robert D. Beckmann, Jr. My gratitude goes also to the Julia Morrow Rogers Memorial Fund for its financial contribution and to James M. Rogers for his belief in the project. Completion of the book was also made possible, in part, by the Indiana Arts Commission and the National Endowment for the Arts, a federal agency.

INDIANA DEPARTMENT OF NATURAL RESOURCES

INDIANA DIVISION OF HISTORIC PRESERVATION AND ARCHAEOLOGY

Indiana Arts Commission
Connecting People to the Arts
This activity made possible, in part, with support of the Indiana Arts Commission, and the National Endowment for the Arts, a federal agency

PREFACE

*"The essential 'State Park' character . . .
provides psychological escape and relaxing atmosphere . . ."[1]*

The complete story of all the various types of state lands in Indiana upon which public recreation is practiced would require several volumes. This study concentrates on the state parks alone. Offering a preservationist point of view, it focuses on evolving policies and attitudes, while examining changes over time in landscape and built environment, and the definition and perception of what constitutes a state park in Indiana.

The definition of a state park varies considerably around the country. By the end of 2000, for example, Indiana had but 23 state parks, while neighboring Michigan boasted nearly a hundred (ranging from vast, relatively pristine acreage in the Upper Peninsula to city beaches along Lake Michigan.) Each state administers what it defines as its state parks differently, making comparisons nearly impossible. Indiana proclaims the purpose of its state parks is to maintain "extensive areas of a native landscape type, with recreational activities appropriate to that setting," a statement sufficiently loose to allow considerable flexibility in interpretation.[2]

The story of the development of state parks in Indiana has always been one of expansion upon, seldom rejection of, older ideas, based upon continual reinterpretation of the original mission statement crafted by the "Father of Indiana State Parks," Richard Lieber. For decades his "primary purpose" for the state parks appeared boldly on trail maps and park guides, asserting that these lands are

> preserving for posterity typical primitive landscapes of scenic grandeur and rugged beauty. . . . [I]t is to be expected that the average citizens will find release from the tension of their overcrowded daily existence; that the contact with nature will refocus with a clearer lens their perspective on life's values.[3]

Definitions of appropriate development—and to what extent—have evolved with the administration's rereading of that statement over the years, shaped by many factors, public clamor and budgetary priorities foremost.[4] Under Lieber's direction, park development in the 1920s initially tended to be minimal, although popular demand led to more. "Contact with nature" was the dominant guideline, and preservation of woodlands a primary consideration. With the coming of the New Deal in the 1930s, development in the parks increased and expanded in order to allow more people to use them, but still mostly in traditional ways, such as picnicking and hiking. In the decades since World War II, changing concepts of leisure and recreational pursuits have increased demand for more parks, more space developed within them, and a greater range of activities offered, even while clinging to older values espousing nature's restorative power.

Notions of what comprise suitable and necessary recreational facilities in state parks today often include such amenities as Olympic-size swimming pools and tennis courts (although precursors of these appeared in a few state parks as early as the 1920s). The once-rustic inns have become almost luxurious, with accommodations for conferences and game rooms for teenagers. Brown County recently installed a family aquatic center in its formerly primitive Abe Martin

iii

Lodge. Construction of these kinds of facilities, along with the ever-increasing number of visitors to state parks, threatens the natural environment that the Division of State Parks continues to declare it is "preserving for posterity." The problem of too many people trying to make contact with a circumscribed patch of nature has no easy solution. In the early 1990s, Pokagon reconfigured its campgrounds with the intention of providing a more pleasant experience for its users, replacing the park's previous attempts to squeeze in as many campsites as possible. Even though today there are far fewer campsites available, public response to the change was generally positive, and some other parks have followed suit with their campgrounds.[5]

Even more so than in the past, many visitors view state parks merely as facilities for outdoor recreation, and encounters with nature are almost incidental. Perhaps because modern life has become so hectic and so saturated with stimuli, what some perceive as contact with nature may simply be sitting outside a recreational vehicle amidst the sparse trees of a crowded campground. Changing patterns in the pursuit of leisure threaten not only the natural landscape, but also the historic architecture of the parks—and what it represents. Unlike some of the recent structures built in the parks, the styles, types, and locations of buildings constructed in the pre-World War II years represented esthetic choices intended to suggest and be suitable to a primitive natural landscape. Indeed, that was the stated intent of the New Deal projects of the 1930s, and that work, which still dominates the pre-World War II parks, has begun to be appreciated and recognized in recent years. Several of these structures in Indiana state parks are now listed in the National Register of Historic Places.[6]

As for preserving particularly significant patches of natural landscape, the program of **nature preserves** initiated in the 1960s seeks to address that problem. Nearly all of the state parks have some area set aside as a nature preserve within their boundaries, most often a forest or wetland. Societal values have continued to change; common environmental attitudes of the turn of the twentieth century, for example, were scarcely acknowledged in the 1930s.[7] No doubt people who come to the parks today regard them differently than visitors did eighty or fifty or thirty years ago, but the *idea* of escaping back to nature remains strong. Today's encounters are as likely to be through the windows of a massive, air-conditioned recreational vehicle as on foot with a backpack slung over the shoulders, and the state parks uneasily attempt to accommodate all. The fitness movement of recent years created a clamor for mountain bike trails, which have been constructed in several of the parks. In order to keep its users happy, the Division of State Parks in the past two or three decades increasingly felt compelled to provide family entertainment in addition to enlightening programs specifically tied to nature or park history. Some people come to the parks expecting to be entertained; budget cuts have made this difficult. Volunteers today fill many of the gaps.

Other State Recreational Lands

Through its many divisions, the Department of Natural Resources oversees several kinds of lands that are open to some form of public recreation; these include state forests, state recreation areas, and fish and wildlife areas, all of which have undergone their own transformations over time. Often the most popular destinations for people wishing to "experience nature" are not state parks at all, but **state forests**. Acres of mature forest fit the popular conception of what a state park looks like, and the distinctions are blurred in the public mind.[8] Morgan-Monroe State Forest, for example, close to Bloomington and less than an hour's drive from Indianapolis, is much used for hiking and picnicking. There are differences in rules and administration; state forests regularly allow hunting in season, while state parks do not. State forests are administered by the Division of Forestry, which still regards them as tree reservations. Lumbering is permitted, although with far more restrictions than in previous years; indeed, despite the fact that the forests originally were set aside largely as future sources of lumber, removal of trees today often meets with considerable protest.

State recreation areas (SRAs) might be considered the opposite end of the outdoor recreation spectrum. Far from pristine nature, almost all are located on flood control reservoirs where motorboats are permitted. The relationship of SRAs to state parks is complicated by their shared history in the 1950s and 1960s and by their shared administration today. The fact that some present state parks were originally called SRAs and in one case, a present SRA (Lieber) was first dedicated as a state park only adds to the confusion. Until recently most state recreation areas had fallen under the jurisdiction of the Division of Reservoir Management, but came back under the auspices of the Division of State Parks in 1996.[9] A few are administered by the Division of Forestry; these are closer to state parks in appearance and function.[10]

Fish and wildlife areas were originally called game preserves, which the Division of Fish and Game [today, Fish and Wildlife] established for the management of wildlife, such as the propagation of pheasants and the raising of raccoons, practices long since abandoned. One of Indiana's present state parks, Ouabache, started life in the 1930s as the Wells County Game Preserve, and a portion of Brown County State Park was originally a game preserve also. Conversely, the former Kankakee State Park straddling the Lake-Newton county line is now the LaSalle Fish and Wildlife Area. One may still picnic and hike there, but the property is geared more toward hunters and anglers.[11]

Largely in the context of historic preservation, this study explores the development over time of Indiana's state park system, concentrating on the built and natural environments and changing perceptions and policies. Other state recreational lands are not examined in this work, including the area known as White River State Park, as it is an atypical urban property controlled by its own appointed commission, not by the Division of State Parks and Reservoirs. Since each park boasts its own unique history both apart from and within the framework of the system, each separate property merits an individual chapter, which follows the narrative history.

 NOTES

1. "Indiana State Parks System Plan." (Indiana Department of Natural Resources [henceforth cited as DNR], Division of Outdoor Recreation, Planning and Special Studies Section, 1984), 27.

2. Quotation from *Ibid*. To compare systems of parks in other states, see, for example, Claire V. Korn, *Michigan State Parks: Yesterday Through Tomorrow* (East Lansing: Michigan State University

Press, 1989); Susan Flader, *Exploring Missouri's Legacy: State Parks and Historic Sites* (Columbia: University of Missouri Press, 1992); Rebecca Conard, *Places of Quiet Beauty: Parks, Preserves, and Environmentalism* (Iowa City: University of Iowa Press, 1997), and Stephen Cox, *The Park Builders: A Comparative History of State Parks in the Pacific Northwest* (Seattle: University of Washington Press, 1988). An early work published by the National Conference of State Parks in its first decade of existence compares the differences in origin, administration, and management policies among many state parks systems; see Beatrice Ward Nelson, *State Recreation: Parks, Forests, and Games Preserves* (Washington, D.C.: National Conference on State Parks, 1928).

3. The statement appears as early as the mid-1930s on individual trail maps distributed at the parks. Examples may be found in the individual State Park Clippings Files at the Indiana Division, Indiana State Library (hereafter stated as ISL).

4. See "State Parks System Plan," 25.

5. Interview, Greiff with Gerald J. Pagac, Director, Division of State Parks, 3 February 1993. (Transcript on file with the Indiana Historical Society, hereafter called IHS.) Conversation with Pagac, 24 January 2003.

6. While the Division of State Parks has been very supportive of the nominations, most have been initiated by organizations and individuals outside DNR, often CCC veterans. The author wrote the nominations for the CCC Recreation Hall/Nature Museum, the Stone Arch Bridge, and the Entrance and Gatehouse at McCormick's Creek; the Combination Shelter at Pokagon; Tepicon Hall at Tippecanoe, the Pokagon State Park Historic District, and the Shakamak State Park Historic District.

7. Later in his life, Aldo Leopold was one of the few voices in the 1930s presaging a holistic ecological philosophy; see especially Leopold, "The Land Ethic," in *A Sand County Almanac* (Oxford: Oxford University Press, 1949). See also Flader, *Thinking Like a Mountain: Aldo Leopold and the Evolution of An Ecological Attitude Toward Deer, Wolves, and Forests* (Columbia: University of Missouri Press, 1974).

8. Interviews, Greiff with Pagac, and Greiff with Jack Costello, Deputy Director, DNR (along with Patrick J. Ralston, Director of DNR), 26 January 1993. (Both transcripts on file with IHS.)

9. In 1996, in a sweeping executive decision motivated primarily by financial concerns, the Division of State Parks and the Division of Reservoir Management merged. In addition, some lands adjacent to each other or in close proximity were placed under the same manager, essentially uniting some properties that formerly were administered by separate divisions.

10. The state recreation areas within state forests are Deam Lake and Starve Hollow. They are managed similarly to state parks in terms of water use and camping. Wyandotte Woods (and Wyandotte Caves) had been similarly administered, but in 2004 it became O'Bannon Woods State Park.

11. Interview, Pagac.

INDIANA STATE PARKS

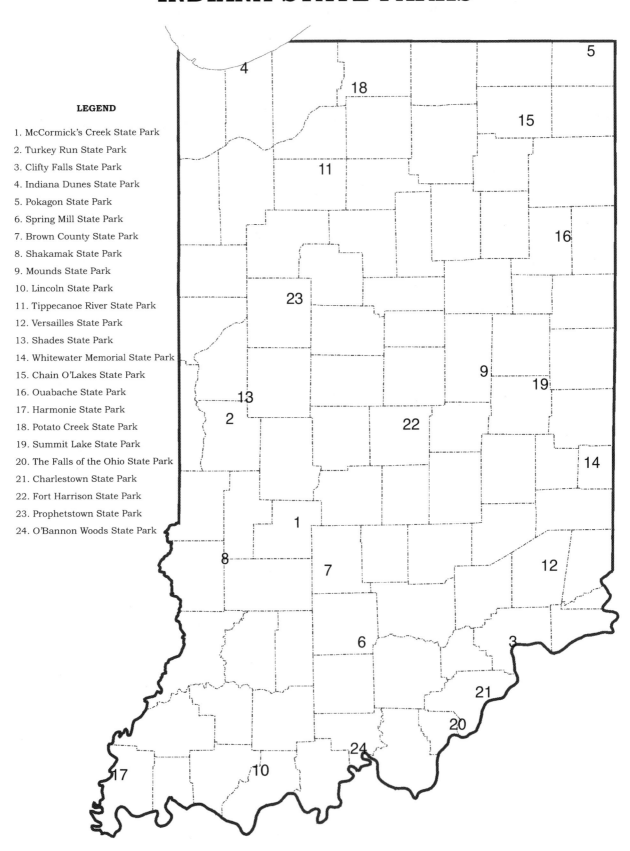

LEGEND

1. McCormick's Creek State Park
2. Turkey Run State Park
3. Clifty Falls State Park
4. Indiana Dunes State Park
5. Pokagon State Park
6. Spring Mill State Park
7. Brown County State Park
8. Shakamak State Park
9. Mounds State Park
10. Lincoln State Park
11. Tippecanoe River State Park
12. Versailles State Park
13. Shades State Park
14. Whitewater Memorial State Park
15. Chain O'Lakes State Park
16. Ouabache State Park
17. Harmonie State Park
18. Potato Creek State Park
19. Summit Lake State Park
20. The Falls of the Ohio State Park
21. Charlestown State Park
22. Fort Harrison State Park
23. Prophetstown State Park
24. O'Bannon Woods State Park

ORGINS

ORIGINS

"havens for our errant, searching souls"[1]

In the decades after the Civil War, a nascent conservation movement emerged across the United States that concerned itself with a variety of issues involving forests, fish and wildlife, water, and wilderness. Doubtless most Americans, if they thought about such things at all, continued to accept that the land and its resources were meant to be used and that the highest use was toward the increase of material production and stimulation of economic growth. But in the minds of a few came the realization that the nation's natural resources, although extensive, might well be finite. Resources such as timber had been rapidly and wastefully exploited for decades by private interests with government sanction, and the furious pace showed little sign of easing. Water conservation started to gain some attention in the late nineteenth century, especially where industrial pollution was diminishing the fish population, which threatened both the livelihood of commercial fishermen and the sport of anglers. A sense of impending and actual loss impelled the conservationists of the nineteenth century, the majority of whom were from the rapidly urbanizing eastern portion of the United States.[2]

Conservation was by no means a unified movement. Most advocates probably shared a range of values but differed in where their chief priorities lay. Some historians have attempted to divide conservationists into two distinct and mutually exclusive camps. Certainly many advocates stressed wise use and resource management for the sake of good husbandry and future availability, while others sought to preserve areas of wild scenic nature for its moral and spiritual value. Supporters at the far end of each view often found themselves in heated opposition. Variously interpreted beliefs, such as those embodied in the writings of essayist Henry David Thoreau, Sierra Club founder John Muir, and countless others, held that contact with nature was important to the physical, mental, and spiritual well-being of Americans living in an increasingly urban society.[3] Such notions became immensely popular as the twentieth century loomed and ultimately inspired the formation of citizen groups that clamored for government-administered parks and forests.[4]

The first national park, identified as a specific area of unique natural beauty to be preserved for the wonder and enjoyment of future generations, was Yellowstone, established by an act of Congress in 1872. Eight years earlier, the federal government had granted the spectacular Yosemite Valley to the state of California for use as a public park. By act of Congress in 1890 Yosemite became a national park with

An 1880s view of the awe-inspiring Yellowstone Canyon by the pioneering photographer F. Jay Haynes.

collection of GJ Greiff

the conscious mission of protecting this tract of wilderness. For the most part, early support for state parks sprang out of similar sorts of nature preservationist movements on a local level. New York, far ahead of most of the nation, in the early 1880s created its first state park to preserve an area around Niagara Falls and a forest reserve in the Adirondacks. Michigan and Minnesota also began to set aside tracts of scenic land in this decade.[5]

Those advocates of parks with wider conservation interests looked upon undeveloped nature, "scenery" untainted by the hand of man, as another resource crying out for protection, akin to water, timber, and minerals. Supporters of protected lands realized their more esoteric values lacked broad support and emphasized other valid reasons for reserving undeveloped areas. For example, in New York, advocates of preserving a portion of the wild Adirondack Mountains stressed the need to secure the watershed to guarantee continued agricultural production, cheap transportation on the state's canals and rivers, and inexpensive power.[6]

Hikers of another day strode forth in constricting garb. The Shades, ca. 1905. *Division of State Parks archives*

The Progressive Era dawned in the 1890s with a cry for government reform and an accompanying crescendo of social activism and public spirit that characterized nearly the next three decades. The conservation movement took on a professional dimension with emphasis on efficient utilization based on scientific principles, largely influenced by the nation's Chief Forester, Gifford Pinchot. Continuing efforts at wilderness preservation sometimes came into conflict with ideas of development of public land and resource management.[7] The latter included such activities as reforestation, flood control efforts, predator eradication, and the establishment of fish hatcheries and game farms.[8]

Advocates of modern forestry pushed for government-administered lands where resource management could be practiced by professionals and a supply of timber, water, or other resources would be assured for future generations. Congressional acts of 1891, 1897, and especially 1905, which placed the administration of national forests with the Department of Agriculture, established federal reserves out of land already under government control, mostly in the West. The Weeks Act of 1911 allowed the federal government to acquire land from private owners for such reserves, which aided the establishment of national forests in the eastern United States.[9]

The spirit of the Progressive Era provided the intellectual and political framework for broader public support of national and state parks throughout the United States. With the creation of Yosemite, General Grant, and Sequoia national parks—all in California—in the 1890s, the national park movement gathered momentum, culminating in the establishment of the National Park Service (NPS) in 1916. The American Civic Association and the American Society of Landscape

Architects were among the most vocal supporters of a system of national parks along with thoughtful planning that stressed the preservation of natural landscapes and development harmonious with the native terrain and vegetation. From the beginning of NPS, landscape architects helped set standards of "consonance with the topography and landscape unity" that trickled down to the state parks, ultimately epitomized by the work of the Civilian Conservation Corps in the 1930s, which was supervised by NPS.[10]

Several states, most of them in the East, began to set aside state parks in the 1890s, although few actually established frameworks for statewide systems that early. After the turn of the century, the movement for state parks gained strength as public demand for them grew, resulting in 1921 in the organization of the National Conference on State Parks. Its mission was "to urge upon our governments . . . the acquisition of land and water areas suitable for recreation and preservation of wild life . . . until eventually there shall be public parks, forests and preserves within easy access of all the people of our nation."[11]

The Progressive Era spawned related movements for organized recreation, some of which blended social welfare with public parks. As a greater percentage of the population lived in cities far from what was widely perceived as the benign influence of nature, an increasing number of people realized the need for places of play–for both children and adults.[12] With this need in mind, some states began to set up their park systems placing the concept of outdoor recreational areas foremost. At the first National Conference on State Parks in 1921 there was even a movement for "A State Park Every Hundred Miles" (regardless of scenic or historic merit) across the country, mindful of the convenience of automobile tourists, which many states adopted to some degree.[13]

At first largely a plaything of the wealthy, the automobile started to become widely accessible to the general public during the 1910s. People were eager to take a spin for purpose or pleasure in their Model T or other vehicle, but the condition of such roads as there were was generally appalling. Some private companies organized regional "highways" to meet the demand for better roads, but it was not until after World War I that either the federal government or most states became involved in highway building and road improvement. The whole face of leisure changed as Americans typically scrambled into the family car to drive toward any seemingly likely destination— or merely for the joy of the drive itself. Frequently farmers headed toward town, but city dwellers invaded the rural countryside in droves, forever changing the landscape. As one Hoosier in the 1920s told the Lynds in their landmark sociological study *Middletown*, "[W]hat's changing this country? I can tell you in just four letters: A-U-T-O!"[14] Indeed, because of the dominance of the automobile, the development of decent roads and interconnecting routes became a crucial factor in assuring access to and therefore the success of newly established state and national parks. People had to be able to get to them— in their cars.[15]

Early twentieth century folders such as these inspired many tourists to visit the national parks. *Collection of GJ Greiff*

The seeds of Indiana's conservation movement sprouted along with those of the rest of the country, but growth was slow at first. In 1881 the Indiana General Assembly approved the establishment of a state Commissioner of Fisheries to be appointed by the governor. In the 1899 legislative session the office was enlarged to Commissioner of Fish and Game. The focus was on establishing ways to assure a bountiful supply of desirable fish and game for anglers and sport hunters. Also as early as 1881, Charles Ingersoll of Purdue University was publicly exhorting the State Board of Agriculture to take up the practice of forestry, lest Indiana lose all its reserves to the demands of farmers who wanted more cleared land and manufacturers who wanted the wood as raw material. Rather than cut down more trees, Ingersoll urged farmers and others to plant them in abundance, not for any short-term gain but for the future.[16] Commercial interests ruled the day, however, and few Hoosiers listened to such cries in the disappearing wilderness until the turn of the century.

At last, in the midst of growing public concern over dwindling woodlands, the Indiana General Assembly in 1901 created the State Board of Forestry. Although it was heavily weighted with lumber interests, the board did include a professionally trained forester, William H. Freeman.[17] The first state forest was established in 1903 in Clark County as an experimental forestry station as well as a reserve. From this initial action the interest of Hoosier citizens in various conservation-related activities expanded rapidly, especially in the areas of soil and water conservation, flood control, and wildlife management. In response, the Indiana General Assembly passed numerous acts over the next two decades. Governor J. Frank Hanly appointed the first Indiana Conservation Commission at the end of his term in 1908. In 1911 the state legislature passed a bill to establish hatcheries for the propagation of desirable game fish to restock Indiana lakes and streams. Progressive-minded governors of both parties, most notably Samuel Ralston (1913-1917) and James P. Goodrich (1917-1921), appointed several commissions and committees that produced mixed results, depending on how powerful were the forces aligned against change.[18]

In this fertile soil sprouted the seedling idea of preserving natural areas for the public good. As early as 1906 state forester William Freeman declared,

> More and more, as the cities swell, and the pressure of industrial life becomes severer [sic], it is of the highest common concern that nature be safeguarded and encouraged in her beneficent work of building up and sustaining the great world of Recreation, in which care is thrown aside, and cramped limbs, bent shoulders, and weary brains may find freedom and invigoration.[19]

 NOTES

1. Richard Lieber, *America's Natural Wealth: A Story of the Use and Abuse of Our Natural Resources* (New York: Harper and Brothers, 1942), 166-167.

2. The following studies represent a variety of historical perspectives. Some useful general sources for the origins and early development of conservation in America are Susan L. Flader, "Scientific Resource Management: An Historical Perspective," *Transactions of the Forty-First North American Wildlife and Natural Resources Conference* (22 March 1976), 5-10, and Roderick Nash, *Wilderness and the American Mind* (New Haven: Yale University Press, 1967), chapters 6-10. Readings on the roots of the late nineteenth century conservation movement comprise Part One of Nash's *American*

Environmentalism: Readings in Conservation History (New York: McGraw-Hill, 1990). For a brief, well-illustrated overview of the many facets of the early conservation movement by a near contemporary, see Ovid Butler, ed., *American Conservation in Picture and in Story* (Washington: American Forestry Association, 1935). See also Michael Williams, *Americans and Their Forests: A Historical Geography* (Cambridge: Cambridge University Press, 1989), especially chapter 12. Earlier chapters deal with the impacts of lumbering, industrial and agricultural use on Americans' attitudes toward forests. Another useful source that focuses on wildlife is Thomas R. Dunlap, *Saving America's Wildlife* (Princeton: Princeton University Press, 1988), especially Part I, "Foundations for a Wildlife Policy."

3. See, for example, Brooks Atkinson, ed., *Walden and Other Writings of Henry David Thoreau* (New York: Modern Library, 1992); John Muir, *The Wilderness World of John Muir* (Boston: Houghton Mifflin Company, 1976), and Muir, *Steep Trails* (Boston: Houghton Mifflin Company, 1918), which is primarily a compilation of Muir's newspaper and magazine pieces written in the 1870s and 1880s.

4. See Nash, *Wilderness*, chapters 6-10; Peter J. Schmitt, *Back to Nature: The Arcadian Myth in Urban America* (New York: Oxford University Press, 1969), especially chapter 15; Alfred Runte, "Preservation Heritage: The Origins of the Park Idea in the United States," *Lectures 1983: Perceptions of the Landscape and Its Preservation* (Indianapolis: Indiana Historical Society, 1984), 53-75. See also Stephen Fox, *John Muir and His Legacy: The American Conservation Movement* (Boston: Little, Brown and Company, 1981), especially chapters 4, 5, and 10. For an ecological interpretation of late nineteenth century conservation, see Donald Worster, *Nature's Economy: A History of Ecological Ideas* (Cambridge: Cambridge University Press, 1985), especially Part 4; also, Nash, *The Rights of Nature: A History of Environmental Ethics* (Madison: University of Wisconsin Press, 1989), especially chapter 2; Fox, *John Muir*, chapter 11.

5. See Raymond H. Torrey, *State Parks and Recreational Uses of State Forests in the United States* (Washington, D.C.: National Conference on State Parks, 1926), especially 19-26; Nelson, *State Recreation*, 1928, 3-5; and Runte, *National Parks: The American Experience* (Lincoln: University of Nebraska Press, 1979), especially chapters 2-4.

6. See Nash, *Wilderness*, 116-121; Runte, *National Parks*, 57.

7. The fight over Hetch Hetchy in California perhaps best represents the conflict. Although set aside as part of Yosemite National Park, in 1913 Hetch Hetchy Valley was granted to the city of San Francisco for use as a reservoir basin by an act of Congress. The bitter battle pitted John Muir, the passionate wilderness advocate, against Gifford Pinchot, the promoter of resource reservation and wise use. See Nash, *Wilderness*, 161-181; Fox, *John Muir*, 139-147.

8. See Samuel P. Hays, *Conservation and the Gospel of Efficiency: The Progressive Conservation Movement, 1890-1920* (Cambridge: Harvard University Press, 1959), especially chapter 7; Williams, *Americans and Their Forests*, chapters 12-13, and Fox, *John Muir*, chapter 5. See also Ernest S. Griffith, "Main Lines of Thoughts and Action," in Henry Jarrett, ed., *Perspectives on Conservation: Essays on America's Natural Resources* (Baltimore: Johns Hopkins Press, 1958), 3-10. For an insider's perspective, see Gifford Pinchot's memoir, *Breaking New Ground* (New York: Harcourt, Brace and Company, 1947), especially parts 3-9.

9. *Ibid.*; see also Lieber, *America's Natural Wealth*, 110-115; Flader, "Resource Management," 12-15, and Butler, *American Conservation*, especially 76-81.

10. See Linda Flint McClelland, *Presenting Nature: The Historic Landscape Design of the National Park Service, 1916-1942* (Washington, D.C.: National Park Service, 1993), 5-9, 229-251.

11. Torrey, *State Parks and State Forests*, 25; Nelson, *State Recreation*, 4-5. See also Harold A. Caparn, "State Parks," in Herbert Evison, ed., *A State Park Anthology* (Washington, D.C.: National Conference on State Parks, 1930), 35-41, and Freeman Tilden, *The State Parks: Their Meaning in American Life* (New York: Alfred A. Knopf, 1962), 5-11.

12. A useful, albeit selective, sketch of the simultaneous movements that affected park development from the nineteenth century to the present is Alfred B. LaGasse and Walter L. Cook, *History of Parks and Recreation* (Arlington: National Recreation and Park Association, 1965); similarly, see Ellis L. Armstrong, ed., *History of Public Works in the United States, 1776-1976* (Chicago: American Public Works Association, 1976), chapter 17. See also Foster R. Dulles, *America Learns to Play: A History of Recreation* (New York: Appleton-Century-Crofts, 1965); Schmitt, *Back to Nature*, especially chapter 1, and Jesse Frederick Steiner, *Americans at Play* (New York: Arno Press and the New York Times, 1970), especially chapter 3.

13. See James L. Greenleaf, "The Study and Selection of Sites for State Parks," in Evison, ed. *State Park Anthology*, 70-76. See also Dulles, *America Learns to Play*, chapter 18 ("A Nation on Wheels"), especially 314-318; Tilden, *The State Parks*, 3-9; Steiner, *Americans at Play*, 35.

14. Robert S. Lynd and Helen Merrell Lynd, *Middletown: A Study in American Culture* (New York: Harcourt, Brace & World, 1929), 251.

15. Greiff, "An Overview of Transportation in Indiana: 1890-1940," 1990, historic context prepared for and on file at the Division of Historic Preservation and Archaeology (hereafter cited as DHPA; other copies available at the Indiana State Library and the Indiana University Library). See Dulles, *America Learns to Play*, chapter 18; John A. Jakle, *The Tourist: Travel in Twentieth Century America* (Lincoln: University of Nebraska Press, 1985), chapters 3, 6, 7; James J. Flink, *The Car Culture* (Cambridge: MIT Press, 1975), chapter 6. See also Robert Shankland, *Steve Mather of the National Parks* (New York: Alfred A. Knopf, 1954), 146-162; Lewis Atherton, *Main Street on the Middle Border* (Bloomington: Indiana University Press, 1954, reprinted 1984), chapter 7; James H. Madison, *Indiana Through Tradition and Change: A History of the Hoosier State and Its People, 1920-1945* (Indianapolis: Indiana Historical Society, 1982), 182-189. An informative study exploring the rapid popularization of the automobile in the early twentieth century is Suzanne Hayes Fischer's "The Best Road South: Early Auto Touring and the Dixie Highway in Indiana" (Master's thesis, Indiana University, 1995).

16. Indiana State Board of Agriculture, *Annual Report*, 1880-81, 229-237. See Clifton J. Phillips, *Indiana in Transition: The Emergence of an Industrial Commonwealth, 1880-1920* (Indianapolis: Indiana Historical Bureau & Indiana Historical Society, 1968), 212-223.

17. The first State Board of Forestry also included Dean Stanley Coulter of Purdue, a major contributor to conservation in Indiana, and Albert Lieber, a cousin of the man who was to become the "Father of Indiana State Parks," Richard Lieber. W.H. Freeman, *Bulletin No. 1, Indiana State Board of Forestry, 1901* (Indianapolis: William B. Burford, 1901).

18. For example, after the great flood of 1913, Governor Ralston appointed the Indiana Flood Commission the following year. Information on developments in forestry activities in the state may be gleaned from Indiana State Board of Forestry, *Annual Reports*, 1903-1916, passim. See Annual Reports of Department of Conservation," *Yearbook of Indiana*, (Indianapolis: Burford and Company, 1917), 242-243, 250; 1919, 442-443 (hereafter cited as "Annual Reports" with appropriate year. See also Phillips, *Indiana in Transition*, 212-223, and John Favinger, "Resourceful Gain," *Outdoor Indiana* 49 (February 1984), 28-31; also, Daniel DenUyl, "History of Forest Conservation in Indiana," in Indiana Academy of Science, *Proceedings* 66 (1956), 261-264; "Indiana Lakes and Streams Stocked With Fish from State Hatcheries," *Outdoor Indiana* 8 (August 1940), 15.

19. "Recreation and the Forest," *Sixth Annual Report of the State Board of Forestry,* 1906 (Indianapolis: William B. Burford, 1906).

RICHARD LIEBER AND THE BEGINNINGS OF INDIANA STATE PARKS

*"havens of rest, comfort and relaxation
for fools like you and me"*[1]

Among Hoosiers who favored conservationist policies and the preservation of tracts of undisturbed natural landscape, Richard Lieber (1869-1944) stood out and ultimately became recognized as the "Father of Indiana State Parks"—a name that scarcely begins to suggest his legendary status. German-born Lieber came to America as a young man, having been steeped in the Romantic literature of several nations and positively saturated in history. A voracious reader throughout his life, Lieber's interest in works of philosophy, religion, and history was no doubt furthered by the cultural atmosphere and discussion groups in the Turnverein, the center for German-American society in Indianapolis. Concepts found in the works of German Romanticists such as Schiller and Goethe are evident in Lieber's writings. Time and again he speaks of the restorative powers of nature, particularly the forest, in a restless and unfriendly world:

Richard Lieber (1869-1944)

stock photo

> The stabilizing influence of the forested places, of nature's grandeur, of a serene landscape, is more essential to the public in these turbulent times than ever before. . . . To spend one afternoon in the open; to tramp over trails in the woods to some lovely or awe-inspiring phenomena of nature for a day . . .to sleep one night under canvas above some rocky gorge—is worth the effort of driving the fifty miles from the city . . .[2]

Other personal qualities one may attribute to Lieber often sound stereotypically German: his pragmatism, for example, or his analytical ability. Both of these characteristics, along with his broad vision, helped him bring far-ranging and complex ideas to fruition. Lieber's abhorrence of waste easily found an appropriate expression through conservation practices.

Lieber was spurred by an especially strong sense of civic and social responsibility. No doubt the reformist atmosphere of the Progressive Era, which was beginning around the time that the young immigrant reached Indianapolis, did much to encourage this tendency. And, too, the Turnverein urged good citizenship. It was not long before Lieber involved himself with various municipal affairs. His work during the 1890s as an arts critic for the *Indianapolis Journal* gave him name recognition in the community; his successful business career in the bottling industry after the turn of the century placed him in a position of some influence.[3] Although Lieber's conservation leanings were virtually innate, he did not publicly enter the arena until the 1900s. Lieber was instrumental in bringing the fourth (and last) annual meeting of the National Conservation Congress to Indianapolis in 1912 and chaired the local Board of Managers for setting up the convention. The National Conservation Congress was an outgrowth of the National Conference of Governors called by President Theodore Roosevelt in 1908 to discuss and implement conservation ideas and policies. Its first annual gathering was in Seattle in the summer of 1909.[4]

Lieber frequently advocated the preservation of parcels of natural landscape for historical reasons and later would repeatedly employ similar arguments to substantiate the value of state parks. Seeing these fragments of pre-settler native forests (or what was generally believed to be such) as historic artifacts from an Indiana that no longer existed, Lieber initially urged the establishment of state parks as a fitting commemoration of Indiana's first century, which was soon to be celebrated in 1916. While he felt the parks offered the public lessons in conservation that were equally important, the properties—or "natural monuments," as Lieber called them—stood

> not only as landmarks of our State's history, not only as those of the entire West territory out of which Indiana was carved, but they will, with their ancient rocks, dells, and giant trees, continue to preach a silent but mighty sermon to generations yet unborn of the struggles, hopes, and ambitions of pioneer days.[5]

Thus he early promoted the idea that setting aside park lands was a form of historic preservation, that the land itself was a historic document of sorts. Later Lieber also advocated saving significant structures and sites as state memorials, which ultimately came under the same administration as state parks.[6]

In the early 1910s, Lieber discussed his ideas for a state park system among his social, business, and political acquaintances, including Samuel Ralston, elected governor in 1912. Numerous people had become interested in establishing one or more state parks in honor of Indiana's approaching centennial. Among supporters in government was state geologist Edward Barrett, who urged the preservation of "regions of picturesque natural scenery for State Park purposes."[7] Barrett tirelessly lectured on numerous specific natural areas in Indiana that he believed suitable to be set aside as state parks, many of which did ultimately achieve that status.

At the same time, many other like-minded citizens were advocating preservation of particularly cherished pieces of land in their local regions. In 1915 the sandstone canyons of Turkey Run in Parke County had come up for sale, but the survival of this relatively pristine natural area was seriously in doubt. The Hoosier Veneer Company coveted the heavily forested site in order to harvest its massive hardwoods. Alarmed, writer Juliet V. Strauss of nearby Rockville began a vigorous campaign to save the beautiful spot and its patch of primeval forest. She contacted Governor Ralston, who appointed a Turkey Run Commission in 1915. Lieber learned of the endangered property from his friend Richard Smith, the editor at the *Indianapolis News*, to which Juliet Strauss regularly contributed. Lieber consulted with the governor about preserving the property and promoted his notions of a state-administered park system. The Turkey Run Commission's original members were Strauss, William Watson Woollen of Indianapolis, and Vida

Newsom of Columbus. Ralston added Lieber to the group in January 1916; the commission was absorbed into the State Park Committee later that year.[8]

The idea of a state park system drew wide public support. Early in 1916 Ralston appointed Lieber to his recently created Indiana Historical Commission, whose purpose was to devise appropriate activities and memorials for the state's centennial celebration that year. Within two months the commission named Lieber chairman of its new State Park Memorial Committee, charged with acquiring and preserving tracts of Indiana's surviving "wilderness" for the inspiration of future generations and as permanent memorials in "gratitude to the pioneers." Besides the Turkey Run Commissioners, members of the new committee included Leo M. Rappaport (Lieber's brother-in-law), Dr. Frank Wynn, and Sol S. Kiser. Money for acquisition of these "scenic and historic reservations" was to be raised through public subscription to the State Park Fund.[9]

The committee quickly determined to save Turkey Run. Other areas identified as potentially worthy to be state parks included the scenic hills of Brown County and the wild dunelands along Lake Michigan in Porter County, which several groups from Chicago strongly supported as well. But none of these properties became the first state park. That honor fell to McCormick's Creek Canyon, a rocky parcel of beautiful trees and rugged terrain in Owen County that had suddenly come up for sale. With financial help

The Old Log Church at Turkey Run, 1925.

Division of State Parks Archives

from the county, the state purchased McCormick's Creek in May of 1916. Later that year, Turkey Run became Indiana's second state park. Although the Hoosier Veneer Company had indeed bid successfully on the property, public outcry and persistent negotiators persuaded the company to sell Turkey Run to the state only a few months later—albeit at a substantial profit. Much of the purchase money came from the public's donations to the State Park Fund.[10]

The first report of the State Park Committee, published in 1917, concluded with the words of Lieber that essentially became the mission statement of Indiana state parks, that "the chief purpose of state parks is to refresh and strengthen and renew tired people, and fit them for the common round of daily life."[11]

World War I temporarily interrupted the work of the State Park Committee, but in 1919 the Indiana General Assembly passed an act creating the Department of Conservation. Its executive director was selected by a four-member bipartisan Conservation Commission appointed by the Governor. While retaining direct control over state parks, Richard Lieber became the first chief executive officer overseeing all five divisions of the new department: Geology, Entomology, Fish and Game, Forestry, and Lands and Waters, which administered the parks. In 1921 the legislature authorized the formation of a sixth division, Engineering. Lieber's pragmatic approach to administration stressed running the department in a businesslike manner, which meant hiring the most suitable directors for the various divisions regardless of their politics. To draw visitors to the state parks, Lieber, by way of frequent speeches, articles, and press releases, "advertised the scenic possibilities of the state . . . for tourists," which "attracted many people to healthful recreation."[12] His efforts were aided by political cartoonists Garr Williams and Charles Kuhn of the *Indianapolis News*, who did much in the 1920s to popularize the idea of weekend trips in the family auto to visit the state parks.

As overseer of Indiana's conservation policy Richard Lieber exhibited a resource management approach that was typical of the Progressive Era, emphasizing efficient use, replacement, and reclamation. But Lieber's greatest impact and most influential contributions lay in the solid foundation that he, ably assisted in the first critical decade by Lawrenceburg native Charles Goodwin Sauers, built for the state's park policy. Sauers, who had a practical and academic background in forestry and landscaping, left Indiana in 1929 to head the Cook County forest preserves outlying Chicago. Much has been added but little of Lieber's underlying philosophy removed over subsequent decades of administration. Indeed, Indiana's parks as organized and developed by Lieber brought the state and its parks administrator into national prominence. In the 1920s and 1930s the Hoosier state park system frequently served as a model for the nation of efficiency, solvency, and high standards. As early as 1923, Turkey Run, a "concrete example of a successful state park," was chosen as the site of the Third National Conference on State Parks by that organization's executive committee. Lieber, along with his good friend Stephen T. Mather, the director of the National Park Service, had organized the National Conference on State Parks in 1921. During most of the 1930s Lieber served as its president.[13]

Among the most important administrative concepts that Lieber insisted upon in establishing his organization was that the parks be essentially self-supporting. Almost from the beginning Indiana state parks charged an admission fee, which for many years remained ten cents. The wisdom of this notion came to be particularly demonstrated during the Depression, when many states that had not followed such a plan and had relied solely on their legislatures' largesse were unable to maintain their parks. Lieber also believed that establishing admission fees would help instill in the public the idea of the value of—and pride in—the parks. In Indiana, he argued, "park visitors are citizens who pridefully consider themselves stockholders in a growing concern, not suppliants of charity or political favor."[14] An additional benefit of charging admission was that it provided a means of recording park visitation for planning purposes.

The former Muscatatuck State Park Inn still stands. *photo by GJ Greiff*

Indiana's state park holdings expanded rapidly with the acquisition of Clifty Falls near Madison in 1920; Muscatatuck, the former Vinegar Mills site in Jennings County, in 1921; Pokagon, on Lake James in Steuben County, in 1925; Indiana Dunes in Porter County the same year, and Spring Mill, the forested cave lands and ruins of a pioneer village near Mitchell, in 1927. Lands adjacent to a game preserve established five years before in Brown County became a new state park in 1929.

Most were gifts to the state conveyed all or in part by local governments. For example, the acquisition of the Failing estate on Lake James that formed the initial tract of Pokagon State Park came about through an act of the legislature in 1925 "whereby Steuben County could issue bonds . . . to be used for purchase of this particular area and deeded to the state."[15] Later parks were also funded in this manner. But Indiana Dunes was an outright purchase, which Lieber had worked hard to persuade the legislature to approve. Largely because of his persistent efforts, as well as considerable prodding from local interests and Chicago groups willing to donate money for the development of such a park, the state bought a tract of unspoiled dunelands in Porter County in 1925.[16]

The Hamer Mill at Spring Mill State Park, ca. 1935.

Each new property arguably met Lieber's criterion that land comprising a state park should contain natural features of exceptional beauty or rarity, or be of some historic value, which Lieber believed was inherent in a "primitive" natural landscape.[17] By providing places in which the public could wander about and interact with nature, Lieber believed that state parks "would constantly be a great public lesson in conservation and . . . impress upon the public mind that wastefulness of Nature's beauties and treasures is out of harmony with the spirit of the time, progress, and the needs of Indiana's new century."[18]

Under Lieber's leadership, state parks theoretically were kept as "natural" as possible and not extensively developed. Obviously a road or two running through each park was necessary, and the Department of Conservation oversaw the development of hiking trails and a few picnic groves. Prisoners from the State Penal Farm at Putnamville initially provided much of the labor. Campgrounds in the 1920s at first were scarcely more than cleared spaces with pit toilets nearby, and perhaps a water pump, but later some of the parks illuminated their camping areas with electric lights. The state provided residences for the custodians (as the property managers were then called) in the parks, often using existing buildings when available and constructing sturdy cottages when necessary. The department

11

provided inns for overnight accommodations in most of the new parks, again, at least initially, using existing buildings where available. Concessionaires managed the inns, paying the state a fee each year. From the beginning, Lieber believed that visitors needed time to absorb fully the lessons and uplifting experiences that a state park offered, and so established the inns, which were moderately priced and modestly appointed, "in no sense luxurious resorts."[19]

Along with the physical and spiritual benefits to be derived from a visit to the state parks came the idea that the public might wish to be—indeed, should be —educated as well, so as to better understand nature. In the mid-1920s some parks offered "nature guides" available at least part time to lead hikes and give illustrated talks. Some of the guides set up small natural history exhibits, usually in the inn lobbies. In large outdoor pens, Pokagon State Park displayed live bison, elk, and deer, all of which had disappeared from the wild in Indiana.

Despite strong verbal commitment to prohibiting all but "natural" activities —as opposed to organized sports or amusements—a few of the parks began to offer more sophisticated forms of entertainment. Tennis courts appeared at Turkey Run in 1927 near the inn. In the late 1920s band concerts were a popular feature at McCormick's Creek and at Pokagon. McCormick's Creek also offered the first swimming pool in a state park; however, it was essentially intended as a replacement for the less satisfactory swimming accommodations in the creek, which had sufficed for the first few years.[20] Lieber had asserted in 1925 that "amusement devices, or standardized sports, have no place in a state park." Only four years later, he hinted his discomfort at the implied conflict between those who seek the enjoyment of nature for its own sake and those who prefer "more vigorous sports . . . swimming, golfing, tennis, speedboating, horseback riding, and dancing." Yet now, while he still would not "overstress these secondary sporting facilities," Lieber would not necessarily exclude them.[21]

Other than provisions for accessibility into the parks and clusters of development in "defined service areas," the overall landscape was little altered. The heavily wooded and creek-laden terrain of Clifty Falls, for example, was largely undeveloped except on the property's south end in the vicinity of the inn, the first of which was adapted from an existing farmhouse. The not-so-pristine orchards and fields that comprised much of Pokagon likewise were initially left alone to "naturalize." The glacially

The old stone farmhouse that was renovated into Clifty Falls State Park's first inn.

collection of Tom Hohman

formed Lake James, so characteristic of northern Indiana, was the primary reason for establishing the park. Parks that offered swimming facilities had proven to be especially desirable to the public, so the Department was eager to acquire more.[22]

As Richard Lieber had noted as early as 1919, "the popularity and usability of any park is in direct proportion to its accessibility."[23] In most cases, the state parks were some distance away from sizable towns or major transportation routes; their isolation was largely the reason many of the tracts had remained relatively unscathed. Visitors to the parks during their first decade of existence often took the train to the nearest depot, then reached the property via horse-drawn conveyances over rugged lanes. Coinciding with Indiana's busy acquisition of state parks was the development of a network of state roads. Originally created in 1917, Indiana's State Highway Commission did not begin to set up a system of state highways until the 1920s. By then, in the midst of the nationwide mania for the automobile, the commission could not hope to keep up with the growing need for new roads and improvement of old ones—but they continued to try, nonetheless.[24]

In keeping with Richard Lieber's interest in history and its accessibility to the public as a source of patriotic inspiration, the legislature in 1925 provided for acquisition of significant historical properties as well as state parks under the aegis of the Division of Lands and Waters. Prior to this time Indiana had established three sites as state memorials or monuments, which now came under Lieber's purview: the Tippecanoe Battlefield near Lafayette, the first state Capitol at Corydon, and the Nancy Hanks Lincoln gravesite. In that same year the General Assembly designated the James F. D. Lanier mansion in Madison as a state memorial, and four years later it awarded similar status to the Pigeon Roost Monument in Scott County, commemorating the massacre of a pioneer settlement. The same division administered both state parks and state memorials until 1970.[25]

The Great Depression gripped the United States during the years following the stock market crash of 1929. The need for recreational facilities grew more acute because of the abundance of forced leisure time brought on by rising unemployment. Lieber avowed that the "stabilizing influence of the forested places, of nature's grandeur, of a serene landscape is more essential to the public in these turbulent times than ever before."[26] The notion of the restorative power of the great outdoors continued to hold wide appeal, accompanied by a growing public interest in active pursuits in open spaces. In the midst of a demoralizing depression, going for a drive was perhaps the most popular form of inexpensive recreation. Families continued to pile into their cars and flocked to the parks over roads that in many cases were still barely improved.[27]

In the early 1930s Indiana admitted four additional parcels to its park system. Three of these properties appeared to stretch the stated standards a bit thin, but they proved to be harbingers of the continually expanding mission of the state parks. Mounds near Anderson had been a privately developed recreational and amusement park, but the primary reason for the state's interest was the historic value of the property's aboriginal Indian mounds. Bass Lake, although an attractive and refreshing body of water, hardly seems exceptional. Still, the state accepted just under ten acres in Starke County to create Bass Lake State Beach, assuring continued public access to one of the state's largest glacially formed lakes and adding to the Department's accommodations for water recreation. Most significantly, the inclusion of Shakamak near Jasonville foreshadowed the Department's later interest in acquiring property strictly for recreational purposes. Largely because the surrounding area, economically hardhit because of played-out coal mining, had an acute need for such a facility, Lieber accepted it as an "experiment." Shakamak is an attractive and heavily forested site today, but in 1930, when it opened as a state park, much of the parcel was a wasteland amidst abandoned mines.[28]

The last state park established under Lieber's directorship was Lincoln in Spencer County, which contained a number of historic sites pertinent to the boyhood of Abraham Lincoln. Assisting Lieber was Paul V. Brown, who also served as executive Secretary of the Indiana Lincoln Union. (Brown later headed the midwest district office of the CCC.) Nancy Hanks Lincoln's gravesite was considered part of the property but continued to be administered as a state memorial. In order to preserve the sanctity of the Lincoln cabin site and grave memorials, the state acquired considerable adjacent acreage southward to be used for picnicking and camping.[29]

Movements for urban parks and organized recreation that had arisen during the Progressive Era now assumed a greater urgency of social welfare in the bleak Depression years, especially programs that offered inner-city children opportunities for healthful exercise in the clean, invigorating air of the country. Such ideas influenced developments in the state parks. The idea of group camps would soon come to full fruition under the New Deal, but in the early 1930s both McCormick's Creek and the newly opened Shakamak offered such facilities for the use of youth organizations such as 4-H. The camps proved very popular.[30]

With the exception of the reclamation work necessary at Shakamak, development of state parks otherwise continued mostly as it had in the 1920s: some trails, a few access roads, a handful of picnic shelters, additional primitive campgrounds, and expansion of some of the park inns. For some time, however, Lieber had been aware of the need for overnight accommodations that lay somewhere between tent camping and the park inns, which, by popular demand, had gradually incorporated more amenities than originally intended. With a hint of regret the Annual Report for 1932 noted that "in spite of ourselves refinements crept in until now we even have hot and cold running water in the rooms and rag rugs on the floor." Lieber first attempted the "Housekeeping Cabin Experiment" at Brown County, where in 1932 the Department constructed twenty such cabins of varying sizes on Kin Hubbard Ridge, along with the Abe Martin Lodge as a gathering place and park center. At the same time, since Shakamak was being developed virtually "from scratch" in the heart of an area hard-hit economically, the Department also built six family cabins overlooking the new lake there. These housekeeping cabins were offered at modest weekly rates so that the average working-class family might "enjoy a summer home for that period."[31]

The Abe Martin Lodge in the 1940s.

Collection of GJ Greiff

14

By 1933 Indiana boasted twelve state parks. All but Muscatatuck and Bass Lake, today administered by Jennings County and Starke County, respectively, remain in the system. Lieber had envisioned these parks as "a mecca of the family of small means and high thoughts, truly the majority in our state."[32] Certainly attendance in the parks grew continually during the early Depression, from 479,009 in 1930 to 622,554 in 1932.[33] Thus the foundation was firmly in place for the New Deal work programs to step in and make the parks more accessible to more people. The original mission statement did not change. But public demand and the New Deal would further stretch that statement's interpretation and means of fulfillment.

 NOTES

1. Lieber, "Annual Report," 1927, 645.

2. Lieber, "Conservation Report," 1932, 364. The Romantic movement in Europe had its greatest support in the British Isles and in the German states, where the concept of *der heilige deutsche Wald* (the holy German forest) was widely celebrated.

3. Greiff, "Richard Lieber: Dreamer and Doer" (unpublished manuscript 1991). See Robert Allen Frederick, "Colonel Richard Lieber, Conservationist and Park Builder: The Indiana Years" (Ph.D. dissertation, Indiana University, Bloomington, 1960), 4, 10, 12-16; Theodor Stempfel, *Funfzig Jahre unermudlichen Deutschen Streben in Indianapolis, 1848-1898* (Indianapolis 1898), chapter 8 (not paginated).

4. See "Conservation Report," 1919, 373, and Frederick, "Lieber," 74-79, 99-106. See also Favinger, "Resourceful Gain," 30-31. For more information on the National Conference of Governors and the National Conservation Congress, see Hays, *Gospel of Efficiency*, 122-141.

5. Lieber, "Report of State Park Committee," *Yearbook of Indiana, 1917*, 495.

6. The administration of state parks and memorials remained in the same division until 1970, when a separate division was established. See "Annual Report of the Department of Natural Resources," (hereafter cited as "DNR Report" with appropriate year) 1970, 1.

7. Edward Barrett, *Indiana Department of Geology and Natural Resources, 41st Annual Report, 1916* (Fort Wayne 1917), 10. See also the *40th Annual Report, 1915*, 9.

8. "Report of State Park Committee" (1917), 496-497; Emma Lieber, *Richard Lieber, by His Wife, Emma* (Indianapolis 1947), 80-81. See Frederick, "Lieber," 115-118; "Struggles of Founding State Park System Recalled," *Indianapolis News*, 1 December 1941; "Hoosier Conservationist: Juliet Strauss," *Outdoor Indiana* 11 (May 1944), 8-9. See also Ray E. Boomhower, *The Country Contributor: The Life and Times of Juliet V. Strauss* (Carmel IN: Guild Press, 1998). See later chapter on Turkey Run State Park for more information on its origins.

9. Quotations from "A System of State Parks," *Indianapolis News*, 23 March 1916. See "Report of State Park Committee," 496-497; "Silver Anniversary of State Parks Is Celebrated With Dinner at Turkey Run," *Outdoor Indiana* 9 (January 1942), 13; E. Lieber, *Richard Lieber*, 81-88.
Numerous letters supporting Lieber's efforts to establish state parks, including examples from such notables as Thomas R. Marshall and James Whitcomb Riley, are on file at the Lilly Library, Indiana University. (See Richard Lieber Manuscripts, Box 1, 1916 folder.)

10. See *Ibid.*; "Richard Lieber Heads State Park Committee," *Indianapolis News*, 18 March 1916. See also Phillips, *Indiana in Transition*, 220-223. See later chapters on the individual histories of McCormick's Creek and Turkey Run for more information on their acquisition and development.

11. "Report of State Park Committee," 498.

12. "Conservation Report," 1926, 286. See "Conservation Reports," 1919, 370-371, 374-375; 1921, 208-209, 215. See also Favinger, "Resourceful Gain," 32-33, and "A Time of Progress," *Outdoor Indiana* 49 (March 1984), 28-29, and Frederick, "Lieber," 143-146, 183-191, 195.

13. "Conservation Report," 1923, 677. See *Proceedings of the Third National Conference on State Parks* (1923). See also Lieber, "Administration and Maintenance of State Parks," *American Planning and Civic Annual* (1936), 187-193; Charles G. Sauers, "Some Principles of State Park Management" in Evison, ed., *State Park Anthology*, 130-133; Tilden, *State Parks*, 8-9, 23-24.

14. Lieber, *America's Natural Wealth*, 171. See Nelson, *State Recreation*, 77-78; and Nelson, "Administration and Administrative Organization" in Evison, ed., *State Park Anthology*, 128. See also Favinger, "Time of Progress," 29-30; Frederick, "Lieber," 194-195.

15. "Conservation Report," 1925, 399-400.

16. *Ibid.*, 399; see Favinger, "Time of Progress," 29-31. Information on state park acquisitions in the 1920s gleaned from "Conservation Reports," 1920-1930, passim.

See later chapters on Clifty Falls, Pokagon, Indiana Dunes, Spring Mill, Brown County, and former parks (Muscatatuck) for more information on the acquisition and development of these lands.

17. Lieber expresses this mission in statements and subsequent actions regularly in "Conservation Reports," 1917-1928. See, for example, "Conservation Report," 1923, 671, in which Lieber declares "a state park in Indiana consists of an area of natural landscape . . . preferably having within its boundaries an unusual and grandiose scenic feature." See also the discussion of "what is a state park" (focusing on Lieber's views) in Tilden, *The State Parks*, 8-12. The ideas of prominent park planner Frederick Law Olmsted's [Jr.] were similar; see, for example, his "Bases for the Selection of State Parks" in Evison, ed. *State Park Anthology*, 67-69.

18. Lieber to Indiana Historical Commission, Indianapolis, 25 November 1916, quoted in David M. Silver, ed., "Richard Lieber and Indiana's Forest Heritage," *Indiana Magazine of History* 67 (March 1971), 54.

19. "Conservation Report," 1926, 358. Cumulative information on the nature and extent of Indiana state park development in this era gathered from "Conservation Reports," 1925-1931, passim.

20. Information on specific examples found in "Conservation Reports," 1925, 323; 1927, 645, 649.

21. See "Conservation Reports," 1925, 323; 1926, 360; 1929, 238.

22. Examples cited from "Conservation Reports" 1925, 322-323; 1926, 358; 1927, 645-647; 1928, 242.

23. Lieber, "Conservation Report," 1919, 438-439.

24. See Greiff, "An Overview of Transportation ," 21-27. See also Fischer, "The Best Road South," especially 12-16, and James H. Madison, *Indiana Through Tradition and Change: A History of the Hoosier State and Its People, 1920-1945.* (Indianapolis: Indiana Historical Society, 1982), 182-192, 336-337.

25. Information on acquisition of memorials from "Conservation Reports," 1925, 389-392, and 1929, 256.

26. "Conservation Report," 1932, 364.

27. Greiff, "Parks for the People: New Deal Work Projects in Indiana State Parks" (M.A. thesis, Department of History, Indiana University, 1992), 24. See Lynd and Lynd, *Middletown in Transition: A Study in Cultural Conflicts* (New York: Harcourt, Brace & World, 1937), 265-269, and Madison, *Indiana Through Tradition and Change*, 184-191.

28. Information on park acquisitions during the early years of the Great Depression is gathered from "Conservation Reports," 1929-1932, passim. See also Tom Wallace, *Over the River: Indiana State Parks and Memorials* (Indianapolis: Department of Conservation, 1932), especially 42-43.

See later chapters on Mounds, Bass Lake, and Shakamak for more details on the acquisition and development of these individual properties.

29. See "Conservation Report," 1932, 368. See later chapter on Lincoln State Park for further information on the acquisition and subsequent development of this property.

30. See "Conservation Report," 1930, 539, and 1932, 370-371. See also Schmitt, *Back to Nature*, chapters 9-10, and Steiner, *Americans at Play*, 43-45.

31. Quotations taken from "Conservation Report," 1932, 364-366. Information on the type and extent of construction in the state parks in the early depression years gathered from "Conservation Reports," 1930-1932, passim.

32. "Conservation Report," 1921, 213.

33. "Conservation Reports," 1930, 436; 1932, 265.

THE NEW DEAL ARRIVES

"an atmosphere satisfyingly, refreshingly close to nature"[1]

3 On March 21, 1933, newly elected President Franklin D. Roosevelt sent a message to Congress proposing "to create a Civilian Conservation Corps to be use in simple work, not interfering with normal employment, and confining itself to forestry, the prevention of soil erosion, flood control, and similar projects. . . . More important, however, than the material gains, will be the moral and spiritual value of such work."[2] Ten days later Roosevelt signed the bill creating Emergency Conservation Work (ECW), popularly known from the outset by the president's original moniker for the program, the Civilian Conservation Corps (CCC). A few years later Congress made the name official. For all practical purposes, the terms are interchangeable.

Unusual cooperation among several branches of federal government eased the program's speedy implementation. The U.S. Army handled the logistics of setting up and maintaining the camps and, along with the other armed forces, provided camp commanders. The Department of the Interior, through its National Park Service (NPS), covered work in national and state parks. NPS offered guidelines for park projects and buildings constructed by the CCC and other agencies under its aegis.[3]

For some years prior to the New Deal, the National Park Service had been developing and compiling designs for public buildings on recreational lands that would "appear to belong to and be a part of their settings." Toward that end, NPS printed several series of plans intended to be executed in the native materials of a particular park. Thus, while a specific type of building in one location might resemble its counterpart in another, they were never identical. The guidelines were sufficiently broad so as to encourage great variation in local interpretation, as long as the finished building harmonized with its surroundings. In

Former camp bugler blows reveille at the 1994 Reunion of CCC Co.556 at Pokagon State Park.

photo by GJ Greiff

17

its time, this style was generally termed "rustic" and originated in the early Arts and Crafts movement, the lodges of the Adirondacks, and the work of urban park pioneer Frederick Law Olmsted, Sr.[4]

Another significant product of Roosevelt's first hectic one hundred days was legislation creating the wide-ranging Federal Emergency Relief Administration (FERA), which included a rudimentary work relief program under its umbrella. FERA director Harry Hopkins soon became head of the Civil Works Administration (CWA), a short-lived program initiated in the fall of 1933 to provide jobs over the coming winter. After the CWA's demise in March 1934, some work relief projects continued under FERA until Roosevelt introduced the Works Progress Administration (WPA) in 1935. This vast program created jobs of all sorts that attempted to match the skills of the unemployed, but that would not compete with whatever jobs the private sector might be able to offer. No doubt the successive Democratic administrations in Indiana during the New Deal years helped WPA programs flourish in the Hoosier state.[5]

In the same election that ushered Roosevelt into the presidency, the people of Indiana in 1932 elected Democrat Paul V. McNutt (1891-1955) governor. Handsome as a matinee idol, McNutt, previously dean of the Law School at Indiana University and national commander of the American Legion, skillfully turned his myriad connections into political success. Taking office in January 1933, more than two months before his national counterpart, McNutt immediately set out to restructure the state government. Among other things, he established the Governor's Commission on Unemployment Relief (GCUR), which created a framework for receiving, administering, and distributing statewide the benefits of federal relief and work programs that were soon to come under Roosevelt's New Deal. McNutt's undersecretary, Shelbyville native and former newspaper editor and publisher Wayne Coy (1903-1957), directed the agency.[6] The Indiana Department of Conservation quickly set up both FERA and CWA work projects, some of which were located in state parks, such as the fish rearing ponds at Shakamak for stocking the new artificial lake (also begun under FERA) on the property.[7]

McNutt's immediate reorganization of the state administrative branch into eight divisions had major consequences for state parks. The Department of Conservation, until this time still headed by Richard Lieber, became a section of the gargantuan Department of Public Works. The governor suspended the Conservation Commission by executive order and named political ally and close personal friend Virgil M. Simmons (1893-1958), a lawyer from Bluffton, the public works administrator as well as the Commissioner of the Department of Conservation, which remained split into six divisions. McNutt appointed Lieber the director of the Division of State Parks and Lands and Waters, which reduced his authority considerably. Also, political patronage replaced merit in the filling of many positions in the Division. Dismayed, Lieber resigned in July 1933, but he continued to play a prominent role nationally working for the cause of state parks until his death in 1944.[8]

Closely supervised by Simmons, Myron L. Rees (1897-1968) served as director of state parks for the next five years, during which the parks saw a flurry of New Deal construction activity. (Rees left the directorship to become the first manager of the new Spring Mill Inn.) His successor was former park engineer

18

Charles DeTurk, who maintained his position until the end of World War II. The Department's stated mission continued to follow closely that which had been laid down by Richard Lieber. As president of the National Conference of State Parks, Lieber in 1936 praised Simmons's work and his taking "adequate advantage of the offers to finance developments which have come from the federal government"—an obvious reference to the CCC and WPA.[9]

To bring the public into closer contact with the Department of Conservation, McNutt and Simmons established the State Conservation Advisory Committee and encouraged the formation of local Conservation Clubs throughout the state (many of whose clubhouses were constructed as WPA projects.) Starting with 37 clubs in 1933, in seven years the number had zoomed to over a thousand. Indiana was divided into sixteen conservation districts. Local clubs elected a representative for each county, and these in turn chose district

Many hungry young men gained weight and muscle with ample good food provided in the CCC dining hall.

Pokagon State Park archives

representatives. These sixteen, along with the state president of the Izaak Walton League (a national organization championing the outdoors) and the state conservation chairman of the American Legion, with which Governor McNutt maintained strong ties, comprised the State Conservation Advisory Committee. The group met quarterly with officials from the Department to discuss conservation problems in all areas. The clubs were instrumental in spreading the gospel of conservation to Hoosier citizens. Besides engaging directly in such activities as the rearing and release of game birds and fish, conservation club members gave talks, sent press releases, sponsored radio programs, and worked with farmers. While the clubs had little direct effect on state parks, they did much to raise public awareness of and interest in conservation generally.[10]

In May 1933, scarcely more than a month after President Roosevelt had signed the bill creating Emergency Conservation Work, Hoosiers acquired their first CCC camp in Morgan-Monroe State Forest, under the United States Department of Agriculture. Within the same month, the National Park Service began supervising Indiana's first CCC projects in state parks at Spring Mill and Lincoln, soon followed by companies at Turkey Run, McCormick's Creek, and Indiana Dunes. Companies generally comprised about two hundred men, and each camp usually housed one company. Camps were racially segregated. Visitors to parks where the CCC was at work tended to consider the camps a tourist attraction and made a point of stopping by.[11]

The CCC was set up as and remained a program geared toward unemployed young men, but the National Park Service also hired older skilled workers from the areas surrounding the camps as foremen and instructors. LEMs, as they were called, routinely served in the CCC in Indiana, where they made important contributions toward sturdy and attractive construction in the parks, such as the fine split-rock masonry work at Pokagon. "LEM" was an acronym for Local Experienced Men or Local Employable Men—the various government documents and primary sources differ. Later, local WPA workers were employed to similar purpose.[12]

Boys of CCC Company 556 outside the barracks at Pokagon.

Pokagon State Park archives

After the appearance in the spring of 1933 of another Bonus Army in Washington, Roosevelt introduced another variation into the CCC. This group of World War I veterans believed that Roosevelt would be more sympathetic to their needs than former President Hoover had been in the summer of 1932. In that well-documented incident, some twenty thousand jobless veterans and their families had come to Washington seeking immediate payment of their combat bonus money. They set up a tent city on the Anacostia Flats south of downtown and were forcefully driven out with tear gas, infantrymen, and tanks under the command of General Douglas MacArthur and his aide, Major Dwight D. Eisenhower.[13] The following spring, once again unemployed veterans of World War I had come in protest seeking their bonus money; this time, they left with the offer of conservation work in the CCC. Many accepted, and ultimately about ten percent of CCC workers were veterans. Their camps were set up separately and work was geared to their age (mainly early thirties to mid-forties) and presumably higher skill level. Indiana's first CCC company composed of veterans established a camp at Brown County State Park and Game Preserve in late 1933.[14]

With the combination of federal programs and state support, Indiana's Department of Conservation undertook and maintained a comprehensive planning and development program in the state parks throughout the 1930s. Under the New Deal, a social-minded "parks for the people" philosophy advocating greater access for all to the great outdoors filtered through the administrations of McNutt and his successor Clifford Townsend (McNutt's lieutenant governor) to the state parks. The Department of Conservation still trumpeted the original mission; park brochures of the period continued to carry the message that the parks were "parts of 'original America' preserving . . . typical primitive landscapes of scenic grandeur." Why were these tracts being preserved? Because, according to the brochures, "contact with nature will refocus with a clearer lens their [the citizens'] perspective on life's values."[15] This statement echoed ideas implicit in NPS guidelines, which encouraged projects that maintained the natural character of a park and that would not disturb its flora and fauna. The notion, of course, was also straight from Lieber and many wilderness advocates of the Progressive Era.[16]

So, the image of nature unmolested remained, notwithstanding the fact that thousands of workers under New Deal auspices were busily engaged in reshaping landscapes that in many cases had already been altered by agriculture or other previous uses. In creating the appearance of wild nature that people expected to find in the parks, while simultaneously making more of the park properties accessible to more visitors, the New Deal agencies and the Department of Conservation walked a precarious line that required constant reinterpretation of Lieber's mission statement for the parks. The inherent conflict between preservation and recreation interests had not gone unnoticed by those in park administration nationwide. For example, a 1937 NPS publication speaks of "ideologies in conflict with each other;" the notion that "certain areas of natural beauty . . . should be preserved from despoliation" clashes with "the demands of city dwellers for recreational opportunities in the outdoors."[17] Of course, the largest constituency in favor of preservation traditionally was urban-based as well; it was they who experienced the sense of loss most keenly.

Other states, of course, were struggling with the same preservation versus playground problem; the elements of conflict were in place from the start and some states, such as Iowa, attempted to adjust their goals and master plans early on. But Indiana, while noting the potential for discord, seemed largely to ignore it. The Division clung to its original mission statement that spoke primarily of preservation and quiet contemplation, yet continued to make small adjustments and compromises to administer to the noisy throng crowding to come into the parks and play.[18]

Indeed, in the 1930s Hoosiers swarmed to the state parks to walk, hike, picnic, or swim; some lingered in campgrounds or inns on the property or at privately owned accommodations that cropped up nearby. Total state park attendance was 479,009 in 1930. By 1940, it had nearly tripled, with 1,212,449 admissions recorded.[19] Even before the New Deal, continually increasing public use had led to the expansion of recreational development in Indiana state parks well beyond simply preserving a relatively "unspoiled" rural property. Nonetheless, park visitors in the 1930s seemed still to fancy themselves in practically a wilderness, if one may believe numerous articles in *Outdoor Indiana* of the period. During the New Deal, the mission of the state parks to maintain this illusion of primitive nature differed little from that under Lieber's administration; the challenge to park planners was to offer what passed for a "wilderness experience" in Indiana to an ever increasing number of people.[20] As Indiana teacher Straussa Pruitt stated in her master's thesis of 1936, "Whatever else [the state parks] offer the citizen in the physical pleasure of outing, camping, hiking, fishing, nature study, and recreation, their primary mission is the keeping intact and 'unimproved' for all generations to come a part of nature's original domain."[21] And indeed, the State Parks Manual issued by the Department of Public Works the following year began with the statement that "the chief function of [the] Division is conserve for all time to the people of Indiana certain areas of typical Hoosier scenery in its virgin state."[22]

The mission of the Civilian Conservation Corps was the protection and restoration of the nation's natural resources. Perception was especially important in the parks—to restore or maintain the "natural" landscape for the enjoyment and inspiration of the public. CCC enrollees planted thousands of trees, mostly white pine and black locust, but also stands of native varieties, in Indiana state parks. While relatively pristine parks such as Turkey Run were already heavily wooded when acquired, others required reforestation so that they might conform to the proper image of state parks; the illusion of a primitive landscape required a woods. For example, the CCC boys planted several thousand trees throughout Shakamak, an abandoned coal mining area, and at Pokagon, much of which had only recently been orchard and farm land adjacent to a resort lake. But alternatively, the CCC cleared many acres of trees and brush in order to build earthfill dams with concrete spillways. These structures formed bodies of water that served multiple purposes of flood control, a permanent water source for wildlife, and, not incidentally, recreation. These were especially welcome in southern Indiana, which lacked natural lakes. The Division had already noted the popularity of water features in state parks, and so Shakamak, Spring Mill, and Lincoln included the impoundment of reservoirs among their CCC or WPA projects. Projects in parks with lakes, whether natural or artificial, usually included rearing ponds to assure that the waters would be well stocked with fish.[23] Evidently nature was to be maintained according to an ideal of "pristine," rather than left to its own devices and thus run the risk of disappointing the anglers who came to the parks.

Along with the practical benefits of exercise and the spiritual uplift a visit to the state parks offered, the notion of providing educational opportunities continued. Richard Lieber had already introduced the idea; moreover, it fit well with the New Deal's desire to increase the social value of the parks. The nature guide service expanded with more personnel in more parks. They led hikes and gave talks at the inns or around campfires. In several of the parks, New Deal workers built or expanded pens and shelters to display live native animals, some of which no longer existed in the wild in Indiana. Among these were the bison and deer corralled at Pokagon and Shakamak. Although in more recent years deer have been overrunning many of Indiana's state parks, at the start of the twentieth century they had completely disappeared from the Hoosier state. In the late 1930s the Division of Fish and Game began to reintroduce deer into selected areas of Indiana, including the Brown County Game Preserve adjacent to the state park. Several parks offered some sort of natural history exhibit, from mineral displays to mounted birds, usually set up in the lobbies of their inns. Today most of the parks have nature centers situated in separate buildings. The seed was planted in 1935 when the WPA adapted a vacated CCC camp structure at McCormick's Creek State Park into a nature museum. The Department of Conservation touted the new facility, "one of the most complete museums of natural history pertaining to native Indiana," as "a distinct forward step" in public offerings. Today, the CCC Recreation Hall/Nature Museum building at McCormick's Creek is listed in the National Register of Historic Places.[24]

Providing opportunities for public education reflected a social concept much in favor in the 1930s, that of the intelligent use of leisure time. Government work programs embraced the idea, since it gave even greater justification to the projects beyond employment and development of recreational facilities.[25] At Shakamak, the CCC created an educational display using natural features *in situ*. Taking advantage of a drift of exposed coal, the workers constructed an entrance display area of poured concrete in 1934 to help tell the geological story of the region.[26]

With ever more Hoosiers clamoring to get close to nature in their state parks, the Department took full advantage of the New Deal programs. Using a variety of native materials, the CCC and WPA built picturesque gatehouses to draw visitors with hints of the delights of nature beyond the entrance. To provide more accessibility and enlarge visitor capacity throughout the parks, both the CCC and WPA constructed additional roads with culverts and bridges that blended into the landscape. Planners continued to build or expand each property's infrastructure in preparation for further development of recreational facilities. In keeping with National Park

CCC boys work on bridge construction at Dunes State Park.

Pokagon State Park archives

Service guidelines, as well as the foundation laid by Lieber, these systems and their structures usually were located in service areas not open to visitors, or else in unobtrusive settings. Even comfort stations could become charming rustic buildings and were proudly displayed in publicity photographs distributed by the Department of Conservation. With the laying of water lines throughout a park, workers could place drinking fountains wherever needed, some with attractive shelters of rough-hewn timber or whatever seemed best to fit the parks' natural landscape.[27]

With well-planned development it became easier for the average park visitor to enjoy outdoor adventures. The CCC and other New Deal agencies built miles of new hiking trails in state parks with some attention to safety and ease of walking, although by today's standards most of their improvements would be considered inadequate. In the 1930s, park administrators did not need to concern themselves unduly over the possibility of liability lawsuits and expected visitors to watch out for themselves and exercise caution as part of the outdoors experience. The CCC and WPA built hundreds of picnic tables throughout the parks and transformed simple forest clearings into extensive picnic grounds. Larger areas featured attractive shelterhouses of native materials, usually designed so as to allow several families to use the structure at the same time.[28]

In several of the state parks, the CCC and WPA created campgrounds for tents and for the automobile trailers that were coming into vogue. Camping in the state parks was an inexpensive way for many lower-income families to spend a vacation, and planners struggled to meet the growing public demand in the 1930s that scarcely anticipated the near mania for camping that was to come after World War II. Campgrounds offered comfort stations, pumps and drinking fountains, shower buildings, and, with increasing frequency, electricity. People may have wanted to get back to nature, but not without at least a modicum of amenities.[29]

CCC boys completed this beautiful saddle barn at Turkey Run in 1940.

photo by GJ Greiff

State parks had permitted horseback riding in the 1920s for those individuals who brought their own animals to ride. The CCC and WPA opened this activity to the general public by constructing attractive saddle barns and miles of horse trails through the forests of most of the parks. Still, except for inn-centered activities such as tennis, most recreational development expanded upon those traditional activities that involved interaction with the natural environment. At state parks, most visitors expected to enjoy basic outdoor pursuits of hiking, picnicking, camping, fishing, and swimming. Both the CCC and WPA developed beaches and accompanying facilities along any suitable body of water and constructed or adapted boathouses for rentals where feasible. The first annual report of the Division of State Parks and Lands and Waters under its new administration in 1933 emphasized the "Value of Water Features in State Parks" and noted the considerable increase in attendance at parks where a body of water was available.[30] Only two state parks offered swimming pools in the 1930s, and the New Deal agencies did not build any additional ones, perhaps in part to adhere to the stated mission of keeping the parks as "natural" as possible.

With more people coming to the parks, both CCC and WPA workers expanded existing inns or constructed family cabins nearby. The latter, originally touted by Lieber, were consistent with the general ideal of greater accessibility embraced by the New Deal programs. These groups of rustic cabins offered an affordable alternative to the inns for lower-income families. Indeed, since most of the visitors to Shakamak State Park tended to come from the surrounding coal-mining counties, the CCC constructed groups of modest, functional cabins perched above the lake with overnight fees within the reach of most working class families. Brown County, too, offered only family cabins until the 1960s.[31]

Several social-improvement trends came together in the 1930s to promote the idea of group camping as a beneficial experience for youth, especially those from low-income urban areas. The old concept of the restorative, even morally uplifting, powers of nature evolved into social programs aimed at underprivileged city dwellers. For a week or two, groups of children or adolescents under the watchful eyes of trained recreational directors and camp counselors could experience the wonders of nature and reap the benefits of fresh air and healthful

CCC boys enlarging the group camp at Pokagon, 1936.

Pokagon State Park archives

outdoor activity, along with woodcraft training and moral guidance. The CCC and WPA built a number of group camps throughout the state park system and had planned even more before the New Deal's demise at the start of World War II. Generally, established youth organizations, such as 4-H or Boys' and Girls' clubs, leased the camps for most of a season, often subleasing them to other such groups when they were not themselves using the facilities. Some parks had two complete group camps; McCormick's Creek had three.[32]

No new parks came into Indiana's system during the New Deal years, although two areas under federal supervision in the 1930s became state parks shortly thereafter: the Recreation Demonstration Areas (RDAs) at Versailles and Winamac. Initially the U.S. Department of the Interior acquired these properties; the WPA then developed them for public recreational use under direct supervision of the National Park Service. Versailles had a CCC company working on the premises as well. The WPA had begun to develop similar properties in Brown County and Martin County under the auspices of the United States Forest Service, but as World War II loomed, the Navy took over the latter for an ammunition depot (later named Crane).[33] The purpose behind RDAs was to demonstrate the recreational value of agriculturally submarginal land that had proven virtually worthless for farming. The Winamac area in Pulaski County was largely a marshy flood plain along the Tippecanoe River, which seldom kept to its banks. Versailles, in Ripley County, consisted of stony hills surrounding wetlands. Located all around the nation, Recreation Demonstration Areas also allowed the New Deal agencies the opportunity to carve "prototypical state parks" from the ground up. Of the forty-six RDAs throughout the country, two thirds ultimately became state parks.[34]

Development of RDAs by the New Deal agencies was akin to their work in established state parks, although there was more to be done in rehabilitating the sites. More emphasis, too, fell on the development of group camps in the RDAs, which further boosted the social value of these reclaimed properties. Each of Indiana's Recreation Demonstration Areas originally had two separate, complete group camps of substantial capacities. In 1943, by prior arrangement, the federal government turned these properties over to the state; they became Versailles and Tippecanoe River State Parks.[35]

Through its Educational Bureau, the Department of Conservation continued a lively publicity campaign throughout the New Deal years, extolling a visit to any of the state parks as a healthful, inspiring, and inexpensive leisure activity. Besides bombarding state newspapers with well-illustrated public service fillers, the Department of Conservation began the publication of *Outdoor Indiana* in 1934.

Not only did this monthly magazine offer numerous articles on the wonders of the parks and other state lands, but it kept its readers up-to-date on recent highway improvements and the best routes to drive.

With the boom in American manufacturing just prior to World War II, employment opportunities increased. The WPA gradually became unnecessary, and the CCC found it more difficult to maintain complete companies, which played havoc for those state parks just beginning major development projects, especially Lincoln and Indiana Dunes. America's entry into the war at the end of 1941 settled the matter, and the following year both the WPA and CCC officially ended, along with most other New Deal programs.[36]

Yet the New Deal agencies left an outstanding legacy that shaped the land and constructed much of the infrastructure and numerous recreational buildings so closely associated with state parks today. The work of the CCC, and to a lesser degree the WPA and its predecessors, in fifteen of Indiana's present parks still serves unobtrusively to enhance visitors' encounters. In recent years appreciation has grown for many of these structures and several have been restored or renovated. The vast scale and scope of the New Deal projects shaped not only the parks themselves but the public's perceptions of what a park should look like. But Indiana state parks are not unique, rather, they are especially fine representative examples of the national experience. Indeed, as Norman T. Newton asserts in his study *Design on the Land*, throughout the nation "the CCC program sent the state park movement forward a good fifty years."[37] Indiana, along with many other states, has documented the work of the New Deal in parks and other recreational lands, and several properties are listed in the National Register of Historic Places.[38]

CCC Company 556 held reunions at Pokagon for fifty years, 1953-2003.

photo by GJ Greiff

1. *The CCC and Its Contribution to a Nation-Wide State Park Recreational Program* (Washington: National Park Service, 1937), 3.

2. Franklin D. Roosevelt, "Message to 73rd Congress, March 21, 1933," in Samuel I. Rosenman, ed., *The Year of Crisis, 1933*, Vol. 2 of *The Public Papers and Addresses of Franklin D. Roosevelt* (New York: Random House, 1938), 80. Information on Roosevelt's lifelong experimentation with forest management and crop rotation is displayed and interpreted at the Franklin D. Roosevelt Home and Library, Hyde Park, New York (hereafter cited as FDR Library). The papers of FDR pertaining to conservation have been compiled into two volumes by Edgar D. Nixon, *Franklin D. Roosevelt and Conservation, 1911-1945* (Hyde Park: Franklin D. Roosevelt Library, 1957). For a discussion of conservation and the New Deal, see A.L. Riesch-Owen, *Conservation Under FDR* (New York: Praeger Books, 1983) and *The Forest Service and the Civilian Conservation Corps: 1933-1942* (Washington, D.C., U.S. Department of Agriculture, 1986). Some useful, near-contemporary discussions include J.D. Guthrie, "The CCC and American Conservation," *Scientific Monthly* 57 (November 1943), 401-412, and Herman J. Muller, "The Civilian Conservation Corps, 1933-1942," *Historical Bulletin* 28 (March 1950), 55-60.

3. Documents concerning the work of the CCC in Indiana state parks may be examined at the National Archives, Washington, D.C. (hereafter, NA) in Record Group 35, Records of the Civilian Conservation Corps (hereafter cited as RG35), especially E115, "Camp Inspection Reports," and Record Group 79, Records of the National Park Service (hereafter, RG79), especially E37, "State Park File 1933-1947," and E39, "Report of District Officers and Inspectors Concerning State Park ECW." See Albert H. Good, *Park and Recreation Structures*, 3 volumes (Washington, D.C.: U.S. Department of the Interior, 1938). This government publication was such a lavishly illustrated, excellent resource, especially of NPS design philosophy, that it was reprinted in 1990 by Graybooks of Boulder, Colorado. See also John C. Paige, *The Civilian Conservation Corps and the National Park Service, 1933-1942: An Administrative History* (Washington: U.S. Government Printing Office, 1985), 3-6. Many published sources are available on the CCC; among the more valuable (albeit subjective) ones written during the New Deal years are Ray Hoyt, *"We Can Take It": A Short Story of the CCC* (New York: American Book Company, 1935), and James J. McEntee, *Now They Are Men: The Story of the CCC* (Washington, D.C.: National Home Library Foundation, 1940). Among the best secondary studies is John A. Salmond, *The Civilian Conservation Corps, 1933-1942: A New Deal Case Study* (Durham: Duke University Press, 1967); also, Perry H. Merrill, *Roosevelt's Forest Army: A History of the Civilian Conservation Corps, 1933-1942* (Montpelier, Vt.: Merrill, 1981), for its overview and evaluation. Specific to state parks, see *The CCC and Its Contribution* and McClelland, *Presenting Nature*, Chapter 7, "A New Deal for State Parks."

4. Author's fieldwork throughout all state lands of the New Deal period revealed numerous examples of structures on different properties built using the same basic plans but always with some local variation. See "Foreword" and "Apologia" of Good, *Park and Recreation Structures*. The quotation is from the "Foreword," vii. See also George Nason, "Architecture and Its Relationship to the Design of Parks," in National Park Service, United States Department of Interior, *1940 Yearbook: Parks and Recreation Progress* (Washington, D.C.: U.S. Government Printing Office, 1941), 56-58. See McClelland, *Presenting Nature*, especially chapter 2, "Origins of a Design Ethic for Natural Parks."

5. See Greiff, "Roads, Rocks, and Recreation: The Legacy of the WPA in Indiana," *Traces* 3 (Summer 1991), 40-47; also, Greiff, "Making a Better Indiana: WPA, Labor and Leisure," 1981 (revised 1987), on file at the Indiana Humanities Council Resource Center. Works abound, both primary and secondary, explaining and interpreting the New Deal and its plethora of programs. Still perhaps the best and most readable is Arthur M. Schlesinger, Jr.'s *The Age of Roosevelt* (three volumes to date), which unfortunately takes the reader only through the election of 1936. Published by the Houghton Mifflin Company of Boston, the individual volumes are *The Crisis of the Old Order* (1957), *The Coming of the New Deal* (1959), and *The Politics of Upheaval* (1960). Another useful work is Frank Freidel, *Franklin D. Roosevelt: Launching the New Deal* (Boston: Little, Brown and Company, 1973). Among the best primary sources, albeit brief, is Arthur Meier Schlesinger [Sr.], *The New Deal in Action* (New York: Macmillan Company, 1940).

6. A glimpse of the vast scope of the GCUR may be seen in *Recovery in Indiana*, 1934-1936, a monthly newsletter distributed by the Governor's Commission on Unemployment Relief, on file in its entire run at the Indiana Division, ISL. Probably the best overview available on Indiana during the New Deal is Madison, *Indiana Through Tradition and Change*. Chapters 3 through 5 specifically deal with the government and politics of the 1930s in Indiana.

7. A third lake impounded much later at Shakamak inundated the fish rearing ponds. Cumulative information on conservation projects throughout the state completed under FERA and CWA is compiled from numerous articles in *Recovery in Indiana*, 1934-1935, and *Outdoor Indiana*, 1934-1935, along with the writer's field surveys of Indiana state parks, 1990-1995.

8. The original structure of the administration of the Department of Conservation established in 1919 by the legislature was restored in 1941 under Governor Henry F. Schricker. "Conservation Report," 1942, 140.

Richard Lieber died in 1944 while vacationing at McCormick's Creek State Park; his ashes are buried beneath his memorial at Turkey Run. See E. Lieber, *Lieber*, 165-170. See also later chapter on Turkey Run.

9. Lieber quoted in Daniel M. Kidney, "Park Direction Under Simmons Is Paid Tribute," *Indianapolis Times*, December 4, 1936. Lieber also generally praises the CCC's work in *America's Natural Wealth*, 215-225. See also Frederick, "Lieber," 333-341. Cumulative information on construction activity in the parks during the New Deal is gathered from "Conservation Reports," 1933-1942, passim, and RG35, E-115, "Camp Inspection Reports," Boxes 68-72, NA.

10. See "Conservation Report," 1940, 310-311; "Conservation Work Lauded," *Indianapolis Star*, 6 January 1936. See also Louis Hasenstab, "Conservation Awakening," (unpublished manuscript, 1990), 28-29, on file at the Division of State Parks.

The Izaak Walton League, founded in 1922 by a group of anglers and outdoorsmen in Chicago, enjoyed considerable popularity and influence in the Midwest. An excellent introduction to the League is Chapter 4, "Conservation Crusade," of Philip V. Scarpino, *Great River: An Environmental History of the Upper Mississippi, 1890-1950*. Columbia: University of Missouri Press, 1985.

11. See *Indiana District: Civilian Conservation Corps, 1938-1939*, (printed report on CCC camps operating in the state), 10, on file at the Nature Center, Pokagon State Park. Cumulative information on CCC camps in the state parks gleaned from numerous articles in *Outdoor Indiana*, 1934-1942, and "Conservation Reports," 1933-1942. See also Salmond, *The Civilian Conservation Corps*, 135-144.

See later chapter on Spring Mill State Park for an example of two segregated companies operating separately on the same property.

CCC veterans companies occasionally were integrated; examples can be found through examination of RG35, E115, (Camp Inspection Reports), Boxes 68-72 (Indiana), NA.

12. Interview, Greiff with Roger Woodcock, veteran of CCC Company 556, Pokagon State Park, 3 November 1990 (tape on file with author); see Paige, *The CCC and the Park Service*, 42-46, 54; Fred E. Leake and Ray S. Carter, *Roosevelt's Tree Army: A Brief History of the Civilian Conservation Corps* (Jefferson Barracks, Missouri: National Association of Civilian Conservation Corps Alumni, 1987), 3-4.

13. See Schlesinger, Jr., *Crisis of the Old Order*, 256-265.

14. Roosevelt, "Executive Order: Administration of the Emergency Conservation Work," 11 May 1933, O.F. 268, Container 1, FDR Library. RG35, E115 (Camp Inspection Reports), Boxes 68, 72, NA. See later chapter on Brown County State Park for further details on the work of the CCC there.

15. Statement titled "The Intelligent Use of Leisure Time" printed on the backs of individual park brochure/trail maps of the 1930s and early 1940s. Several of these brochures are on file in their respective individual park files in the State Park Clippings Files, ISL.

16. Greiff, "Parks for the People." See Paige, *The CCC and the Park Service*, 44. See Good, *Park and Recreation Structures*, and also McClelland, *Presenting Nature*, 229-233, for further details on NPS guidelines and the CCC.

17. "Leadership and Programs on State Parks," in National Park Service, *1937 Yearbook*, 21.

18. Indiana finally tried to confront the conflict more directly after World War II, which shows up more in statements and studies in the Division's Annual Reports (1944-1964) than in the stubbornly unchanging mission statement that the fabled Lieber had crafted. Other states, whether successfully or not, grappled with preserve versus play earlier; see, for example, Conard, "Hot Kitchens," 442-443, for the situation confronting Iowa state parks in the early 1930s; see also Cox, *Park Builders*, 84-86.

19. "Conservation Report," 1941, 953.

20. Frequent articles in *Outdoor Indiana*, 1934-1940, speak of adventures and encounters with nature. For example, "Traveling the Trails of Clifty Should Involve Side Exploration," *Outdoor Indiana* 5 (June 1938), 12, 18, entices the reader by promising the "feeling of being a real explorer." The mission of the state parks and what visitors expected from them (or at least what the Department of Conservation wanted them to expect) may also be gleaned from contemporary park brochures (filed in the individual park folders in the State Parks Clipping Files, ISL). See Greiff, "Parks for the People"; see also *The CCC and Its Contribution*.

21. Straussa V. Pruitt, "Indiana State Parks—Their Educational Contributions" (M.A. thesis, Indiana State Teachers College, Terre Haute, 1936), 50.

22. "State Park Manual." (Indianapolis: Department of Public Works, 1937), 1.

23. Greiff, "New Deal Work Projects in Indiana State Parks," 1991, historic context on file at DHPA. Cumulative information on conservation work in the state parks was gathered from "Conservation Reports," 1933-1942, passim, and *Outdoor Indiana*, 1934-1942, passim, along with the writer's field surveys, 1990-1995. See Olmsted, "Present-Day Outdoor Recreation and the Relation of State Parks to It," in Evison, ed., *State Park Anthology*, 18-27; Tilden, *The State Parks*, esp. 17-30; McClelland, *Presenting Nature*, 239-232; also, Riesch-Owen, *Conservation Under FDR*.

24. Quotations from "Conservation Report, 1936," 412. See "'Ask the Naturalist,'" *Outdoor Indiana* 13 (June 1946), 6, 13.

25. The conservative press often criticized recreational projects as frivolous; to counter such charges, *Recreation* magazine, published by the National Recreation Association, carried numerous editorial articles in the 1930s in praise of New Deal recreational projects. See, for example,"Ridicule of Recreation," *Recreation* 30 (May 1936), 49.

26. Discontinued many years ago, the former coal exhibit still stands, unidentified, near Trail 2 in Shakamak. Appearing as it does, those who encounter it most likely assume it to be an abandoned mine. A photograph of the exhibit in use appears in "Shakamak State Park Possesses Varied Attractions Centering Around Lakes," *Outdoor Indiana* 6 (August 1939), 16. Construction photographs are located in RG79, E37, Box 40, "Project Reports: CCC in State Parks," NA.

27. Cumulative information on New Deal infrastructure development in Indiana state parks is gathered from "Conservation Reports," 1933-1942, passim, and *Outdoor Indiana*, 1934-1942, passim, along with the writer's field surveys. See "New Deal Work Projects in Indiana State Parks." Many examples from Indiana State Parks are included in Good, *Parks and Recreation Structures*.

28. Cumulative information on picnic facility development in Indiana state parks is compiled from "Conservation Reports," 1933-1942, passim, and the writer's field surveys.

29. Cumulative information on campground development in Indiana state parks is gathered from "Conservation Reports," 1933-1942, passim, and *Outdoor Indiana*, 1934-1940, passim, along with the writer's field surveys.

30. "Conservation Report," 1933, 383. Cumulative information on state park development during the New Deal is compiled from "Conservation Reports," 1933-1942, passim, *Outdoor Indiana*, 1934-1940, passim, and the writer's field surveys. See also "New Deal Work Projects in Indiana State Parks," and Greiff, "Roads, Rocks, and Recreation."

31. CCC monthly reports for Shakamak State Park, RG79, E37 (State Park Files), Box 206, NA. The majority of Shakamak's patrons still come from the surrounding three counties; the number of family cabins has more than tripled, and there still is no inn at the park.

Cumulative information on park inns and cabins is gathered from "Conservation Reports," 1934-1942, passim, and the writer's field surveys.

32. For a time in the early 1960s, McCormick's Creek offered *six* group camps of varying sizes. See later chapter on McCormick's Creek State Park for more details.

Cumulative information on group camps is gathered from "Conservation Reports," 1933-1942, passim; *Outdoor Indiana*, 1934-1942, passim, and the writer's field surveys. There are numerous contemporary sources extolling the benefits of group camping; see, for example, "The National Park Service in the Field of Organized Camping," in National Park Service, *1937 Yearbook*, 38-42.

33. The property in Brown County eventually became Yellowwood State Forest. See Greiff, "New Deal Work Projects on Indiana State Lands," 1996, on file at DHPA.

34. See Phoebe Cutler, *The Public Landscape of the New Deal* (New Haven: Yale University Press, 1985), 70-82, for a discussion of Recreation Demonstration Areas. See also McClelland, *Presenting Nature*, 247-251.

35. "Two State Park Areas Approved," *Indianapolis News*, 25 August 1938; "Two New State Parks," *Outdoor Indiana* 10 (May 1943), back page; Harold L. Ickes, Secretary of the Interior, to Roosevelt, 4 November 1942, concerning the disposal and transfer of RDAs, O.F. 6p, National Park Service, Container 16, 1941-42, FDR Library. Information on Versailles and Winamac RDAs is gleaned from RG79, E47 (Records Concerning Recreation Demonstration Areas), Box 150, NA; also, on Winamac alone, from *Pulaski County Democrat*, 1934-1940, passim. Some information also found in the folders on "Versailles" and "Winamac Recreation Demonstration Area" in the Administrative Files of the Indiana Department of Conservation, R4269, Box 40, "State Parks: Shakamak/Winamac," Commission on Public Records (State Archives), Indianapolis. (Hereafter cited as SA.) See also Conrad L. Wirth, *Parks, Politics,*

and the People (Norman: University of Oklahoma Press, 1980), 176-190; Cutler, *Public Landscape*, 70-82; McClelland, *Presenting Nature*, 249-250. "NPS in Organized Camping" discusses RDAs in relation to group camps.

See later chapters on Tippecanoe and Versailles state parks for further information on their acquisition and development.

36. See Salmond, "A Fight for Permanence," in *New Deal Case Study*, 145-161.

37. Newton, *Design on the Land*, 576.

38. See Greiff, "Parks for the People." See also, for example, the following NRHP multiple property documentation forms: Greiff, "New Deal Resources"; Joyce McKay, "Civilian Conservation Corps Properties in Iowa State Parks, 1933-1942," 1989; and Rolf T. Anderson, "Minnesota State Park CCC/WPA/Rustic Style Historic Resources," 1988. Michigan parks were especially well-served, as evidenced in its CCC camp inspection reports found in RG79, E-40 "Reports of Regional Officers and Inspectors Concerning State Park ECW, 1935-36," Box 1, NA. Among the several published sources that speak of the New Deal in various state park systems, see for example, Flader, *Exploring Missouri's Legacy*, 7-10; and Carol Ahlgren, "The Civilian Conservation Corps and Wisconsin State Park Development," *Wisconsin Magazine of History* (Spring 1988), 184-216.

WORLD WAR II AND POSTWAR EXPANSION

"preserving and conserving the original landscape"[1]

4

With homefront restrictions on automobile use, wartime brought an understandable decrease in state park attendance. Particularly noted was the loss of out-of-state visitors. In the years just before World War II, the number of non-Hoosiers coming to Indiana's well-publicized state parks hovered above forty percent of the total; during the war it dwindled to about ten. The positive side was that this left more of the park facilities available to the people of Indiana, who were less inclined or able to vacation at distant sites and began to explore possibilities closer to home. Several articles in *Outdoor Indiana* trumpeted the message in propaganda-tinged prose that the state had much to offer "even with the Jap-enforced restrictions that have only begun to make themselves felt."[2]

So great was the demand on the inns in the parks that fewer than half the requests for accommodations could be filled, but at least the state park system helped meet the need of the local population to escape. Visitors to several of the parks were often military personnel based nearby or civilian workers at defense plants. This was particularly true of Brown County, McCormick's Creek, and Spring Mill, within reasonable distance from Camp Atterbury, the Martin County (later, Crane) Naval Depot, and the military training center at Indiana University. Indiana Dunes provided a much-needed playground for the workers at the heavy industries of the Calumet region. In addition, many of the hotel rooms in these parks temporarily housed members of the armed forces or defense workers. At times the military requested the use of a state park for various purposes, which the Department of Conservation honored as long as there would be no permanent damage or threat to public safety. In Brown County the Army set up a motor transport training school in the two abandoned CCC camps there. In undeveloped isolated areas of Brown County, Tippecanoe and Versailles, the Army carried on limited maneuvers.[3]

Diminished attendance created a serious loss of income but did allow the most intensively used areas of the parks a "rest." Less money necessitated a reduction in staff, almost a moot point since so many park employees had joined the war effort. For the most part there was no new development and only minimal maintenance of park lands through the war years. In 1943 the state legislature voted funds for the upkeep of the two newly acquired state parks, Tippecanoe River and Versailles, both of which had been fully developed by the federal government, along with the money to complete construction of the dam and spillway at Lincoln State Park. Park personnel were able to finish a few other of the projects that

Tepicon Hall, formerly the dining hall of a group camp at Tippecanoe River State Park, was built by the Works Progress Administration. *photo by GJ Greiff*

31

the CCC or WPA had started but abandoned when the war began, such as the commissary building at Turkey Run and the bath house at Shakamak. (Both buildings have since been remodeled into nature centers.)[4]

With attendance down and minimal funds and manpower to carry on development, the Department had an opportunity to take its time and plan ahead for the postwar years. The tremendous demand for hotel accommodations, for example, indicated to planners a justification for "considerable expansion, both in area and facilities." The Division of Engineering carried out master plan studies for existing parks and geographic investigations proposing new parks for areas of the state not well served. In planning for postwar development, the Department contemplated acquiring more tracts of "outstanding scenic beauty" but added the new mission of establishing recreational lands near populous areas. The goal was to "double the size of the present state park system" and to "provide state park facilities within approximately thirty-five miles of all residents of Indiana." One area considered for many years as a potential site for a state park was the Mississinewa River valley in Miami and Wabash counties, toward which the legislature authorized a survey in 1945. Wolf Lake, a large body of water adjoining Hammond, was under consideration as well, clearly demonstrating the Department's goal of developing park lands near enough to offer escape to residents of urban areas. But neither the Mississinewa valley nor Wolf Lake studies resulted in a state park. The Army Corps of Engineers did eventually construct a reservoir southeast of Peru in the 1960s on the Mississinewa, which offered recreational areas along its shores administered by the Division of Reservoir Management.[5]

As soon as materials became available after the war, the Department of Conservation set out to complete some still-unfinished New Deal projects, as well as desperately needed repair and expansion in several of the state parks. But the postwar years saw trends develop that would forever influence park policy in ways not always harmonious with the mission set forth by Richard Lieber, despite the fact that his statement about parks being "typical primitive landscape" continued to be printed on all their brochures. With the return of veterans and the increase in leisure time available to the average American came the public cry for more places to play and a greater availability and variety of recreational facilities in those places. The Department of Conservation responded quickly. The Shades, a private resort park upstream from and similar in topography to Turkey Run, became Indiana's fifteenth state park in 1947. Public subscription, through the "Save the Shades" campaign, funded the acquisition of some two thousand acres of largely undisturbed oak, pine, and beech forest hovering over twisting sandstone canyons.[6]

But old standards of what constituted an appropriate site for a state park had begun to shift. In 1945 Milton Matter, who had just assumed directorship of the Department of Conservation, flatly stated that "Indiana needs more parks" and went on to cite the Whitewater River valley in the eastern part of the state as "particularly well-suited in all respects to park development." Certainly the region was in need of a state park, since the area had none, but no tract of undisturbed land lay waiting to be preserved. Instead, the Department helped survey a four-county area in search of a suitable site to develop into a state park, which proved to be a location south of Liberty in Union County. Residents of it and the

A peaceful setting overlooking the lake at Whitewater State Park.

photo by GJ Greiff

surrounding counties raised funds to purchase the land and present it to the state to make into a park. According to a contemporary article in *Outdoor Indiana*, the acquisition of Whitewater was a "step in the department's long-range plan to provide a state park within easy driving distance of every Hoosier resident," a concept long practiced in some other states but not in Indiana prior to this time.[7]

An additional dimension to the attraction of state parks in the postwar years was their commercial value in drawing new businesses into Indiana. Speaking about the Whitewater project, Governor Ralph Gates suggested that "it may well be that the balance wheel on industrial postwar relocation will be swung by the recreational facilities a state can offer for the use of a firm's employees."[8] From the movement's beginning, supporters of state parks had often felt compelled to demonstrate concrete practicality rather than abstract esthetics. Esoteric values of spiritual refreshment or even the old "scenery as resource" idea were seldom sufficient; certainly the more ammunition with which to bombard a reluctant legislature to surrender more funds, the better. Throughout the 1950s the idea continued that Indiana's "park chain is regarded as an important asset to the state's humming industry. Good recreation resources mean a more relaxed working force," which "goes far in better relations on the job — in turn keeping up production." Popular also at this time was the concept of the American heritage of the great outdoors, a recycled idea that Richard Lieber had proffered decades earlier.[9]

The problem with increasing the number of state parks to serve all parts of Indiana was, of course, that large tracts of unsullied land, assuming any still existed at all, were far from evenly distributed. Seldom were sizable areas of ready-made parkland situated conveniently near overcrowded cities longing for relief. Something of an exception was Scales Lake near Boonville, a tract of formerly stripmined land developed and partly reforested by the WPA in the 1930s and administered by the Division of Forestry as a nursery and fish hatchery. As the property was less than twenty miles from the city of Evansville, with a sizable lake for swimming and other aquatic pursuits, it now seemed more suitable to make recreation the primary focus. The Division of State Parks, Lands and Waters took over the management of Scales Lake in 1951. Over twenty years before, the Division had noted the importance of access to water to a park's popularity. Scales Lake was Indiana's second state beach (Bass Lake State Beach was the first) and the Division planned to acquire many more, as well as to expand facilities for water recreation in existing parks.[10]

In 1947 the Indiana General Assembly had voted to use half of the funds that earlier had been allocated for creating a state park in northwest Lake County at Wolf Lake for purchase of land and development of the Kankakee River Restoration Project. Its purpose was to preserve some remnant of the Great Kankakee Marsh that once covered parts of several counties in northwestern Indiana. Similar in concept to rehabilitating a historic building, restoring this altered landscape to something approximating its pre-

Fish Hatchery in Scales Lake State Forest, Boonville, Ind.

Fish rearing ponds built by the WPA at Scales Lake in the 1930s.

collection of Tom Hohman

settler appearance may be viewed as another type of historic preservation, motivated by a sense of loss of connection with the past. The Department of Conservation approved an area straddling the Newton-Lake county line as a site for a state park, but it took until 1952 to procure sufficient land and open the property to visitors. Some existing cottages were put into use as housekeeping cabins and the Division soon developed picnic and camping grounds, but despite the park's proximity to the populous Calumet Region, Kankakee State Park was never very popular. There were no facilities for swimming, and the marshland bred swarms of mosquitoes, which the Department attempted to control with DDT.[11]

The Cagles Mill project, the first park development on a flood control reservoir, showed greater promise once arrangements with the Army Corps of Engineers were worked out. Under the federal Flood Control Act of 1938, the Corps acquired land along the Putnam-Owen county line to construct the state's first such reservoir, named Cagles Mill Lake, completed in 1953. While keeping ownership, the Army transferred the administration of the property to the Department of Conservation, which placed it under the Division of State Parks, Lands and Waters in 1956 as Cataract Lake State Recreation Area. Two years later, Governor Harold Handley dedicated the property as Richard Lieber State Park to honor the system's first director.[12] Unlike other state parks, this one permitted motorboating on the lake, while mindful that its primary purpose was still flood control.

The 1950s witnessed a tremendous rise in family camping and thus, an increasing clamor for more campgrounds. The Division found it virtually impossible to keep up with the demand. In the decade that nurtured today's cry for family values, the family vacation was all-important. In part this was due to the increase in leisure time in the postwar years, especially as more and more companies offered longer paid vacations to their employees, who usually were the sole breadwinners for their families. Some recreation planners had assumed that the men who had slogged through World War II would shun the outdoors experience ever after, but apparently nothing was further from the truth. State and national parks everywhere felt the crunch.[13]

Virtually every recreation publication in the 1950s and 1960s noted the phenomenal popularity of family camping. Every annual report of the Division of

State Parks spoke of the need to "close the gap between present facilities and immediate future needs." The number of campsites occupied rose 256 percent in six years, from 1955 to 1961, and continued to grow. Parks struggled to create more campsites in a finite area while still maintaining sufficient space for each family to enjoy the experience. Until the postwar years many of the campgrounds in the parks did not have designated individual sites; in 1962 a policy statement developed to improve campground operation included the establishment of specific sites, basing the maximum number on the availability of sanitary facilities. There was to be no more than one family group per site, and no more families would be allowed in a camping area than there were vacant spots. Still the Division wavered over flatly turning people away; parks were to designate "emergency overflow areas" for temporary camping, preferably in locations identified as possible future campgrounds. Camping facilities ranged from the primitive to those with a degree of modern convenience. Several had centrally located showers and laundry tubs, and some parks provided limited electrical service for each site. Most families brought tents or hauled tent-trailers into the parks, but a growing number lugged self-contained trailers.[14]

The continuing growth of group camps in the 1950s was the state's attempt to meet an apparent social need. Now couched in more acceptable terms for the postwar era, such as "character-building," group camps had first proliferated during the New Deal, and the values behind them harkened back to the Progressive era at the end of the nineteenth century. The Division saw itself as "a State agency with responsibilities to provide camping facilities for youth groups" and so "continue[d] to fulfill its mission" as funding

This amphitheater was constructed in the 1930s between two group camps at McCormick's Creek State Park.

photo by GJ Greiff

allowed.[15] Demand for group camp sites exceeded available accommodations. In 1956 a newly built camp opened at Lincoln, and in the early 1960s adaptive reuse created additional facilities at Indiana Dunes, Shades, and Muscatatuck. The postwar baby boom certainly was one reason for the rise in usage. But thanks in part to the Department's own efforts at public education, as well as the attention aroused by the still-popular local conservation clubs and various youth organizations, interest in the outdoors, nature study, and camping activities flourished. Having helped to create this hungry child, the Department felt obligated to feed it. At their peak in 1965, there were sixteen group camps scattered among eight state parks.[16]

In the postwar years the naturalist service— inaugurated on a part-time seasonal basis with a few "nature guides" in the 1920s— grew increasingly more popular with park visitors. By the 1940s the Division had begun to set some

35

professional standards for its nature guide service, renamed the naturalist service. A weekend pre-season training school acquainted the naturalists with the park system, specific flora and fauna of Indiana, the requirements of the program, and one another. By this time all employees of the service were college students or graduates in biological sciences. The role of the naturalist gradually expanded. While taking visitors on nature hikes and offering lectures and demonstrations about the wonders of the natural world remained at the heart of the job, naturalists increasingly led purely recreational activities and provided wholesome entertainment, such as campfire sing-alongs and square dancing. These activities were added "to create an atmosphere of sociability" and, interestingly, "to develop the recreational use of state parks."[17] Division reports in the 1950s and 1960s asserted that these planned programs "have become a tradition of long standing in the Indiana State Parks, and guests look forward to them." The idea of keeping the public entertained seems somewhat at odds with the Division's stated concept that in the parks the "actual pursuit of recreation is on the basis of self-direction."[18]

By the early 1960s thirteen of the twenty state parks had naturalists on staff full time during the summer months and on weekends during April, May, September, and October. Their role was to "help visitors in our parks have a more enjoyable and satisfying experience because they can more fully understand and appreciate the wonders of nature around them." Educating the public, however subtle the statement, continued to be part of the mission of state parks. As this goal was to be gained not only through traditional nature hikes but also through "constant friendly mingling with visitors," patience and diplomacy were requirements as necessary as solid training in a biological field for a state park naturalist.[19] No doubt an adequate singing voice or proficiency on a musical instrument was a plus. The naturalists had become the Division's links to the public, effectively serving as the parks' public relations agents, which remains true today.

During the early 1960s the Division undertook to evaluate its accomplishments and goals, acknowledging the trends of the postwar years in the state parks. For the first time the Division noted that "parks are developments," suggesting that even the choice of preserving a "natural" area is itself a type of development, part of a manmade site shaped "according to a well designed master plan drawn by qualified park planners."[20] Since the late 1940s the Division had given attention to standards established by the National Conference of State Parks (NCSP) in its "Suggested Criteria for Evaluating Areas Proposed for Inclusion in the State Park System," which listed five types of classifications: 1) State Parks, the traditional areas of "outstanding scenic or wilderness character," and whose value may also be "historical, archaeological, ecological, geological . . . preserved as nearly as possible." 2) State Monuments [State Memorials], limited areas that "preserve objects of historic or scientific interest and places commemorating important persons or historical events." The Division of State Parks still administered Indiana's state memorials and continued to do so until 1970.[21] 3) State Recreation Areas, "selected and developed primarily to provide non-urban outdoor recreation opportunities . . . but having the best available scenic quality," usually located in the vicinity of a city with no traditional state park close by. 4) State Beaches, basically frontage on lakes to provide public access to water recreation. 5) State Parkways, greenways along a non-commercial road usually connecting parks or recreation areas.[22]

One of the several beautiful lakes in Chain O'Lakes State Park.   *photo by GJ Greiff*

In its 1961 Annual Report the Division noted that while the "Indiana state park system . . . had as its first parks . . . areas selected on the basis of their outstanding scenic, geological, historical, or ecological features . . . in recent years some areas were acquired for the purpose of providing recreational facilities, such as swimming, fishing, boating, and similar activities, more so than for the purpose of acquiring an outstanding landscape." The statement is significant because at last the Division openly and consistently embraced the idea of at least some state parks as primarily places of play.[23] Implied but not stated was the need for a body of water on these newer acquisitions. A lake—or the potential for an artificial one—seemed to hold appeal at least as great as beautiful terrain for the park-going public.

Indiana's twentieth park seemed to adhere more to the traditional standards, because Chain O'Lakes was and is an especially fine representative example of northern Indiana terrain. Happily, this meant the land included several spring-fed lakes. Plans for creating this park that would offer respite convenient to the Fort Wayne area had gotten underway in the late 1940s, but legal barriers delayed acquisition for over ten years. Chain O'Lakes State Park was dedicated in 1960; the following year the Division established its twenty-first state park, which also offered ample opportunities for water recreation. The Mansfield Reservoir project was the Army Corps' second flood control reservoir in Indiana. In an arrangement similar to that of Cataract Lake (which became Lieber State Park), the Corps gave over the operation of all recreational facilities to the Division of State Parks. This property, however, was called Raccoon Lake State Recreation Area, not State Park, in deference to the National Conference on State Parks guidelines. People soon swarmed to the new park, whatever it was called, and work began immediately to develop campgrounds, a beach, and boat ramps, for here, as on Cataract Lake, motorboating was allowed.[24]

While their closest ties were to the Department's Division of Fish and Game, conservation clubs remained strong in the 1950s and continued to play a leading role in promoting the outdoors. Among their chief activities, begun in the 1930s, was to raise and distribute the birds hatched on the state game farms. By the 1960s most conservationists had discredited this practice of pen-rearing birds and instead shifted emphasis toward creating more and better natural habitats. The state game farms at Muscatatuck, which then reverted to functioning as a regular state park, and in Wells County near Bluffton, both closed in 1962. The Department transferred the latter property from the Division of Fish and Game, and with the flick of a pen the Division of State Parks acquired a "ready-made park," originally developed from farmland in the 1930s by the CCC and WPA. It was christened Ouabache (the French spelling of the adjacent Wabash River) State Recreation Area, to differentiate it from the more "pristine" state parks, again in keeping with the NCSP guidelines.[25]

The unsteady balance between usage and preservation in the state parks began to wobble precariously as more areas were opened to development, especially for desperately needed campgrounds. Finding suitable space was particularly a problem in the older, more traditional parks. The Division continued to add more land to existing parks whenever possible, and often placed camping facilities and other more intrusive new development into the new tracts. Additional land on the east edge of Spring Mill, for example, offered open space for a

Service building constructed by the CCC at what was then called Wells County State Forest and Game Preserve.

photo by GJ Greiff

purely functional saddle barn that would not impinge on the heavily forested acreage that comprised most of the older parts of the park.[26]

At the beginning of the 1960s, under a new professionally oriented administration overseen by Conservation Director Donald E. Foltz, a former legislative leader, the Division established a series of short- and long-term objectives. Given the success of the Cagles Mill and Raccoon Lake projects, among the goals was the development of several state recreation areas in conjunction with the flood control projects of the Army Corps of Engineers.[27] The Division of Engineering was busily surveying the new Monroe Reservoir, and plans were underway for the future Mississinewa and Salamonie flood control projects. But as the Corps continued to build more reservoirs in Indiana, administration of adjacent recreational lands became more complicated, particularly since restrictions imposed on water use in state parks did not apply to the reservoirs. Starting with beaches at Fairfax and Paynetown, the Division of State Parks for a brief time in the mid-1960s administered the State Recreation Areas on Lake Monroe near Bloomington, but in 1968 these came under the control of the new Division of Reservoir Management.[28]

Through nearly all the years of postwar development, Kenneth R. Cougill, a landscape architect from Anderson, directed the Division of State Parks, Lands and Waters. (It became simply the Division of State Parks in 1957 when other responsibilities having to do with "Lands and Waters" shifted to the new Division of Water Resources.) Originally the Assistant Director, Cougill took over the office early in 1947 from Robert F. Wirsching, who had held the position less than two years. During Cougill's long tenure the Department of Conservation moved twice, first out of the Statehouse to 311 West Washington Street in 1949, then to the sixth floor of the new State Office Building in 1961. His assistant Robert Starrett, a Pennsylvania native with a museum background, took over as Acting Director from the ailing Cougill in 1964.[29]

By the early 1960s the Department of Conservation had grown to ten divisions (each designated as either a Land Holding, Resources Management, or Service Division), which still bore some superficial resemblance to Lieber's original plan. But some divisions had become unwieldy, their responsibilities more complex and often overlapping those of other state agencies outside the Department. By executive order Governor Matthew Welsh, who took office in 1961, put ninety-nine professional positions in the Department of Conservation on the merit system. His appointee Director Foltz spent a good deal of his tenure streamlining and reorganizing within the Department, a prelude to its metamorphosis in 1965 into the Department of Natural Resources (DNR). No doubt largely because of Foltz's former position in the legislature and his prodding, the 1963 General Assembly voted most favorably on matters pertaining to the parks, and allocated money for desperately needed capital improvements, funded largely by a controversial cigarette tax. Parks had long ceased to be literally self-supporting, although admission and other charges still went directly toward upkeep. But the tremendous upsurge in demand for and use of the parks had required almost constant repair, rehabilitation, or new construction, which entrance and other user fees could not possibly cover.[30]

In 1963 the General Assembly passed legislation creating a six-member Indiana Conservation Advisory Committee comprised of three House and three Senate members, with whom the Department would consult on activities in the parks and other Conservation properties and on long-range planning. The state legislature also asked for a ten-year master plan covering acquisition and development, which Vollmer Associates, a New York City consulting firm, completed in the fall of 1964. Among other things the Vollmer Plan pressed for new state recreational lands near five major population centers: Indianapolis, the Calumet region, Evansville, South Bend, and Muncie. The plan also called for considerable expansion of existing parks. The means of financing such a vast and ambitious project would be subject to considerable debate. Still, by this point, few questioned that the demand for more parks had escalated enormously in the postwar years. Not without some alarm at the immensity of the task, the Division struggled valiantly to keep its parks available to all who wished to enjoy them. As the Annual Report had summed up the problem in 1961:

> The need continues to be urgent for increased opportunities for large numbers of our citizens to enjoy the benefits of the out-of-doors. Population increase, transportation improvements, increases in leisure, and income changes are four fueling factors that have moved upward in the past and are likely to continue to move upwards in the future.[31]

 NOTES

1. "Escape Back to Nature," *Outdoor Indiana* 11 (May 1944), 1.
2. "Parks in Wartime Serve Visitors Arriving by Auto, Bus or Train When They Need Relaxation," *Outdoor Indiana* 9 (March 1942), 19, 31. See "Conservation Report," 1943, 761-762. See also, for example, "War, Tire Rationing 'Sell' Hoosiers on State Vacations, Kiwanians Told," *Indianapolis Star*, 30 July 1942, and Arthur P. Tiernan, "Income Tax, 'A' Card Vacation Worries Solved— State Parks Have Everything," *Indianapolis Star*, 4 April 1943.

3. See "Park Inns Deluged With Requests for Room Reservations," news release from Indiana Department of Conservation, 29 June 1944; "Conservation Reports," 1943, 761-762, 766-767; 1944, 862, 866.

4. See "Conservation Report," 1943, 763-764; also, Blueprint, Shakamak State Park Bath House, 25 August 1941, and Application for Commissary Building at Turkey Run, 10 November 1941, also blueprints, 28 February and 6 March, 1941, found in R4269, Box 40, "State Parks: Shakamak/Winamac," SA.

5. Quotations from "Conservation Report," 1944, 862, 905-906; see also 1945, 561; also, *Outdoor Indiana of the Future: Postwar and Long-Range Program*, 1945, prepared by the Indiana Department of Conservation for the General Assembly (on file at the Division of State Parks).

The Division of Reservoir Management merged with the Division of State Parks in 1996. The funds raised to pursue the development of Wolf Lake as a state park ultimately went instead to a site along the southern border of Lake County, which became, for a time, Kankakee State Park. Today it is the LaSalle Fish and Wildlife Area. See later chapter on former state parks for more information on the acquisition and development of this property.

6. See later chapter on Shades State Park for more information on its previous history, acquisition, and development.

7. Milton Matter quoted in "Meet the Whitewater Memorial Park," *Outdoor Indiana* 12 (July 1945), 14; See "Whitewater Memorial— Newest State Park!" *Outdoor Indiana* 16, (January 1949), 6. See later chapter on Whitewater State Park for more details on its acquisition and development.

8. "Meet the Whitewater Memorial Park," 14.

9. Quotations from "Conservation Report," 1960, I-10, I-11. For a typical example of Lieber's views linking patriotism, parks, and conservation, see "Conservation Report," 1926, 291-296.

10. See "Conservation Report," 1951, 7, 10-11. See chapter on former state parks for more information on Scales Lake.

11. See "Conservation Reports," 1947, 673, 713; 1954, 30. See chapter on former state parks for more information on the acquisition and development of Kankakee State Park.

12. See "Building of Cagles Mill Dam Started," Indianapolis News, 2 July 1948; "Cagles Mill: Newest Conservation Acquisition," Outdoor Indiana 16 (October 1949), 6-7; "Cagle Mill Area Transferred to State in Ceremonies June 19," Outdoor Indiana 19 (August 1952), 14; "Conservation Report," 1955, 3; "19th State Park," Indianapolis News, 12 July 1958; "Dedication Program for Richard Lieber State Park," July 12, 1958. See later chapter on former state parks for more details on acquisition and development of Lieber State Park.

13. See, for example, Flader, *Exploring Missouri's Legacy*, 13-15.

14. See "Conservation Reports," 1961, 5-6; 1962, 7, 26-27; "Growth of Family Camping in the Indiana State Parks," *Outdoor Indiana* 28 (January 1962), 15-21; "Indiana Vacation Time," *Outdoor Indiana* 31 (May 1964), 15, 18-21; Thomas B. March, "Space Race . . . By Public Demand," *Outdoor Indiana* 31 (August 1964), 2-5. See also Hasenstab, "Conservation Awakening," 29.

15. "Conservation Report," 1954, 22

16. See "Conservation Report," 1965, 26. See also Hasenstab, "Child Growth Through Camping," *Outdoor Indiana* 19 (April 1952), 15,17; and Hasenstab, "Indiana's State-Owned Youth Camps," *Outdoor Indiana* 28 (June 1961), 27-30.

17. "Conservation Report," 1941, 954.

18. Quotations from "Conservation Report," 1961, 8, 33. See also "Ask the Naturalist," *Outdoor Indiana* 13 (June 1946), 6, 13.

19. Quotation from "Conservation Report," 1964, 24. See also *Ibid.*; Roger Hedge, "Our State Park Naturalists," *Outdoor Indiana* 48 (December 1981-January 1982), 34-35.

20. Statement found in "Conservation Reports," 1961, 8; 1962, 7, *et al.*

21. In 1969. two years after the Indiana State Museum moved from its former location in the basement of the State House to its own building in Indianapolis (the Old City Hall), DNR established a new Division of Museums and Memorials, properties which up until then had been administered by the Division of State Parks. The change took effect 1 February 1970.

22. See guidelines in "Conservation Report," 1961, 2, *et al.* The original list of criteria also included "state waysides." Indiana's system of roadside parks, begun in 1938, was administered by the the state highway department. Roadside parks peaked in the 1960s; few remain today. Greiff, "Havens of the Highways: The Life and Languishing of Indiana's Roadside Parks," (unpublished manuscript, 1994).

23. Statement found in "Conservation Report," 1961, 7-8, and repeated in succeeding annual reports. See chapter 3 for a discussion on Indiana's reluctance to confront openly the preservation versus recreation conflict.

24. See "Noble County Park Suit is Dropped," *Indianapolis News* (6 June 1955); Pat Redmond, "Chain-O-Lakes Couldn't Help Becoming Park," *Indianapolis News* (15 April 1960); Conservation Report," 1960, I-13 through I-15; Henry C. Prange, "The new Mansfield Reservoir and Raccoon Lake State Recreation Area," *Outdoor Indiana* 28 (August 1961), 19-23; "Governor Dedicates State's 21st Park," *Indianapolis Star*, 10 September 1961; Joseph R. Keel, "Raccoon Lake Popular With Hoosier Campers," *Indianapolis Star*, 11 August 1963. See later chapters on Chain O'Lakes and former state parks (Raccoon Lake SRA) for more information on the acquisition and development of these properties.

25. See "State to Get Ready-Made Park," *Indianapolis Times*, 28 December 1961; "Conservation Report," 1963, 8. Also, Hasenstab, former Director of Recreation, Division of State Parks, telephone interview, 15 May 1995. See later chapter on Ouabache State Park for more details on its acquisition and development; also the chapter on former state parks for information on Muscatatuck.

26. See "Conservation Report," 1960, I-62.

27. See "Conservation Report," 1961, 1; Interview, Greiff with Donald E. Foltz, former Director of Indiana Department of Conservation, 9 April 1994. (Transcript on file at IHS.)

28. See "DNR Reports," 1968, 1; 1970, 1. In 1996 the Division of Reservoir Management combined with the Division of State Parks once again, although the differences in administration of each type of property remained.

29. See "Conservation Reports," 1961, 5; 1964, 1; Interview, Greiff with Hasenstab, 2 March 1993. (Transcript on file at IHS.)

30. See "Conservation Report," 1963, 5-6; Interview, Foltz.
See also Favinger, "Time of Progress," 36.

31. "Conservation Report," 1961, 6. See Vollmer Associates, *1965-1975: A Pivotal Decade in Indiana: Master Plan for Acquisition and Development*, prepared for Department of Conservation, 1964 (on file at the Division of State Parks). See "10-Year State Park Expansion Plan Detailed," *Indianapolis Star* (11 September 1964); "Cities May Fight Foltz Plan," *Indianapolis Star* (13 September 1964). See also Favinger, "Environmental Era," *Outdoor Indiana* 49 (March 1984), 26.

THE GROWING WEB OF BUREAUCRACY

"facing new challenges: the problems of success"[1]

In the two decades after World War II several separate state agencies had mushroomed that overlapped into the provinces of the Department of Conservation's various divisions, which themselves had proliferated like amoebae. In an attempt to sort things out, the General Assembly in 1965 established the Department of Natural Resources (DNR), which combined all state agencies having to do with environmental and conservation concerns under one administration. In effect, the old Department of Conservation acquired the Flood Control and Water Resources Commission, the State Soil and Water Conservation Committee, and the Indiana Recreational Council. Instead of the old Conservation Commission, the new agency's board was to be called the Natural Resources Commission, with six bipartisan gubernatorial appointees and six ex-officio members of other departments. The new DNR director was to have two deputy directors, each heading a new bureau: Water and Mineral Resources, and Land, Forest, and Wildlife. Each bureau had a separate bipartisan Advisory Council of twelve members. The new Department of Natural Resources began with fourteen divisions. Nine of these were directed from one or the other of the new bureaus; the Division of State Parks, obviously, came under the Bureau of Land, Forest, and Wildlife. The five remaining divisions were defined as service, for example, Law Enforcement or Public Information and Education.[2] (In the decades since, the organization of the divisions has been expanded, contracted, and rearranged for reasons of efficiency, finances, and politics, so that the DNR of today bears but a slight resemblance to its original plan.)

At first glance the idea of one of those divisions, that of Outdoor Recreation, seems superfluous, surely overlapping the interests of the Division of State Parks as well as others. But the roots of the Division of Outdoor Recreation lay in the Indiana Recreational Council, created only two years earlier in 1963, under the auspices of the State Board of Health to promote healthful recreational pursuits and the development of more public recreational facilities. Under DNR, the Division of Outdoor Recreation was initially set up to receive and disburse money acquired from the federal government through its new Land and Water Conservation Fund (LWCF) that Congress enacted in 1965. This directly affected state parks; money from that fund went toward developing properties and rehabilitating inns and other facilities. Around the mid-1980s, however, LWCF funds shrunk, and Indiana's allotment became insufficient to provide funds for the state parks. Only later at the turn of

A former country lane, now a trail in Harmonie State Park.

photo by GJ Greiff

the millennium did enough money finally became available to the parks for land acquisition.[3]

State parks, of course, are a major component of the recreation studies and plans devised by the Division of Outdoor Recreation.[4] Over the years it revised and expanded upon the original Vollmer Plan for state park acquisition and development, which the General Assembly in 1965 accepted and supported with appropriations for the next two years. Foremost in the master plan was the establishment of state recreational land near five major population centers: Indianapolis, the Calumet region, South Bend, Muncie, and Evansville. As luck would have it, a 700-acre tract of marginal farmland south of New Harmony—within thirty miles of Evansville—was donated for a state park that very year. Even while the state was still buying up land adjacent to the gift parcel, and long before it was completely developed, the Division of State Parks opened the property to the public as Harmonie State Recreation Area (SRA). It was formally dedicated as a state park in 1978. In 1968 the state began to purchase agricultural land east of North Liberty around Potato Creek in southern St. Joseph County for a park that would serve the South Bend region. Potato Creek State Recreation Area officially opened in 1977; it was dedicated as Potato Creek State Park in 1982.[5] For a time in the 1960s and 1970s, the Division used "state recreation area" to differentiate such rehabilitated properties from the "traditional" parks. But by the 1980s, owing partly to the confusion with the SRAs adjacent to reservoirs (which were then administered by a different division), all lands administered by the Division of State Parks were designated "state parks," regardless of their condition and previous use.[6]

Although the region abounds with natural lakes, Worster Lake was created by damming Potato Creek in the 1970s.

photo by GJ Greiff

In 1968 the Natural Resources Commission established the Division of Reservoir Management within the Department of Natural Resources specifically to handle recreation on the several large flood control reservoirs that the Army Corps of Engineers was creating in the 1960s. Dedicated in 1964, Lake Monroe already had four state recreation areas, little more than boat launches and beaches, initially administered by the Division of State Parks. These and newly created recreation sites on the reservoirs at Mississinewa and Salamonie immediately went into the new Division. Eleven years later in 1979, Raccoon SRA on Cecil M. Hardin (formerly Mansfield) Reservoir was transferred to this division from the Division of State Parks, along with the former Lieber State Park (now Lieber SRA). DNR recognized that these reservoir properties were "distinct from state parks [that were] intended to preserve and utilize a natural phenomenon" and needed to be managed differently.[7]

To complicate matters further, the Division of Forestry, which had always allowed some recreational pursuits on its lands, set up park-like sections within some of their properties. Deam Lake State Recreation Area in Clark County was created in 1965 after the completion of a 194-acre lake named for Indiana's first state forester. Wyandotte Woods was established in the middle of Harrison-Crawford State Forest and Driftwood SRA, in Jackson-Washington State Forest.[8]

Beautiful Pine Hills was dedicated as Indiana's first Nature Preserve in 1968.

photo by GJ Greiff

In the decades following World War II, the growing tendency to acquire property based primarily on its location and recreational potential had led to several state parks that strayed from Richard Lieber's original mission of preserving significant natural areas, especially ironic given that his mission statement speaking of "scenic grandeur and rugged beauty" was still printed on all park trail maps through the 1980s.[9] Certain areas especially worthy of note within many of the existing state parks, particularly the older "traditional" properties, were threatened to some degree by increasing usage and demand for more development. In addition, small tracts of unspoiled Indiana terrain sometimes became available to the state that were unsuitable for parks because of their limited size. A looming sense of loss, similar to that which fostered the conservationists of the nineteenth century, impelled many to try to save these scattered patches of unspoiled land. In the 1960s private groups such as the Nature Conservancy had begun to purchase endangered parcels, often forests or wetlands, to ensure their preservation. Responding to all these issues, the Indiana General Assembly passed the Nature Preserves Act in 1967. The following year the first property so dedicated was Pine Hills, a natural area at the east end of Shades State Park that had been given to the state by the Nature Conservancy in 1961. In rapid succession DNR established seven more nature preserves, only two in existing state parks (Donaldson Woods in Spring Mill and Rocky Hollow-Falls Canyon in Turkey Run), the others under the jurisdiction of different DNR divisions and one under private non-profit ownership. To coordinate administration the Department set up a separate Division of Nature Preserves in 1969.[10] Today nearly all the state parks have at least one designated Nature Preserve.

That same year yet another new division, Museums and Memorials, was carved out of the Division of State Parks, effective 1 February 1970. Over the years the number of state memorials had greatly multiplied, and with the State Museum (also under State Parks administration) rapidly filling the spaces of its then-new home in the former Indianapolis City Hall, a separate division was warranted. (In 2002 the Indiana State Museum moved into a sprawling new state-of-the-art facility west of downtown Indianapolis.) Pennsylvania native Joseph A. Blatt, who had become state parks director in 1966 after Robert Starrett's brief stint in the post, moved to head the new Division of Museums and Memorials in 1970. Governor Edgar Whitcomb then appointed G.T. Donceel of the Division of Reservoir Management as Acting Director of the Division of State Parks, until David Herbst (formerly head of the Division of Fish and Wildlife) assumed the post the following year. Having five directors in less than ten years cannot have been conducive to continuity in the Division.[11]

As public needs began to change, the immense popularity of group camps started to decline in the 1970s. Camp Tepicon at Tippecanoe and Hassmer Hill at Versailles were razed, which still left one group camp in each of those parks. Indiana Dunes for a short time in the 1960s had also offered two group camps; one used the old Duneside Inn for its accommodations. Today both camps are gone. From a peak of sixteen group camps in eight parks, the number has dwindled to seven in six parks: McCormick's Creek, Shakamak, Pokagon, Tippecanoe, Versailles, and Lincoln.[12] They are used as much by adults for retreats, conferences, and reunions as by youth groups. Most parks today offer tent camping areas set aside for adult-supervised youth groups, so such organizations do still use the state parks for overnight camping and related outdoor activities. Certainly the upkeep of such areas is minimal compared to that of a group camp's numerous frame buildings, which was a factor in the latter's decline.

SWIMMING POOL, 4 H CAMP, VERSAILLES, INDIANA

This swimming pool, along with the rest of the Hassmer Hill group camp at Versailles State Park, was demolished in 1977.   *collection of Tom Hohman*

Maintenance and repair work in many of the state parks was aided and enhanced by the Green Thumb program, started in 1965, as one of President Lyndon B. Johnson's Great Society domestic aid programs. Sponsored by the National Farmers Union and funded primarily by the United States Department of Labor, Green Thumb offered job placement, training, and part-time employment in community service, often in parks and recreation, for low-income people 55 years and older. Although minimal compared to the impact of the New Deal work programs, Green Thumb (its name changed to Experience Works in 2002) had been helpful in several of Indiana's state parks. Projects began in 1967 and continued into the 1980s to a lesser extent; work ranged from building stone walls at Spring Mill to helping clean up Clifty Falls after tornadoes struck in 1974. Later the workers were more likely to staff nature centers and assist with clerical tasks; the program dwindled and finally ended in the early 2000s.[13]

On the other end of the age spectrum, the federal government began a Youth Conservation Corps (YCC) in the early 1970s that offered summer employment at minimum wage for high school students. Indiana became involved in 1974, administering the program through DNR. Local organizations or governments (school corporations, colleges, counties, municipalities) set up conservation-related work. No YCC camps were actually established in state parks, but enrollees of the project at Tri-State (now Trine) University in Angola constructed and maintained trails at nearby Pokagon. Greatly inspired by the CCC of the 1930s as well the success of the YCC program, Congress passed a measure three years later creating the Young Adult Conservation Corps (YACC) for unemployed youth ages 16-23, who were not in school, to do conservation work. YACC crews toiled in several Indiana state parks, where they did considerable work on trails and some lesser construction projects. Both YACC and YCC ended in 1982 owing to the federal budget cuts of the Reagan era.[14]

Ever mindful of forging good relationships with the public, the Division decided to experiment with an annual entrance permit, since many people visited either the same park or a sampling around the state numerous times throughout the year. The annual pass was offered for the first time in 1967 and was wildly successful—so much so that a second printing of the permits was necessary. Their popularity continued to grow each year; today for a reduced rate a Golden Hoosier Passport is also available for seniors. A study in 1984 showed that retirees were among the fastest growing groups of visitors to Indiana parks.[15]

Instigated by the Natural Resources Commission, the first Buffalo Riders Conference on 23 June 1973 was an attempt by DNR to establish a dialogue of sorts with a portion of the public. The name referred to the bison on the Indiana state seal. Although not as highly structured, the Buffalo Riders Conference was based upon the idea of the old Conservation Advisory Committee of the 1930s. Each spring representatives of most of the DNR divisions presented programs and talks at an all-day conference attended by Indiana outdoors writers, leaders of environmental groups, hunting organizations, and conservationists, creating an opportunity for direct discussion of the Department's current and long-range plans. In practice, however, the largest constituency of state park visitors—families—had no organization promulgating their needs and desires. In part because of this fact, the conference was discontinued in the 1990s. About the time the Buffalo Riders Conference had become established, DNR took to the air waves in an attempt to reach those Hoosier families and began broadcasting a weekly television program statewide called "Indiana Outdoors." Popular with outdoors enthusiasts, the program offered all manner of nature-related topics, often featuring naturalists from the various state parks. Unfortunately, the budget reductions that began in the 1980s ultimately brought an end to the production of "Indiana Outdoors."[16]

With the environmental movement galloping in all directions in the 1970s, it seemed obvious that among the roles of a state park naturalist was to embrace the lofty, if vague, goal to "inspire the visitor to become a better user of the environment."[17] Parks began to set up separate interpretive nature centers, and in 1974 the Division established a chief naturalist and initiated year-round naturalist service at the six state parks with inns (McCormick's Creek, Turkey Run, Clifty Falls, Pokagon, Spring Mill, Brown County). Fulltime naturalists came to Mounds, Potato Creek, and Indiana Dunes in the 1980s. In the 1990s, Lincoln and a new park, Falls of the Ohio, added fulltime naturalists, who are today called *interpretive* naturalists to more clearly define their role. The remaining parks have seasonal naturalists. While doing more structured programs within the parks, year-round naturalists, especially in the off seasons, also go out into the community, giving talks and programs to schools and clubs. Naturalists have for many years been a strong presence each summer at the Indiana State Fair's DNR building as well.

For decades the naturalists have been the parks' most direct link to the public, presenting the parks to the people and "enrich[ing] the lives of those who participate in planned park activities."[18] Among the most popular were the park patch programs, which began in 1974 with the Junior Naturalist patch, designed to acquaint youngsters with nature and perhaps instill an environmental consciousness as well. (Park cleanup and recycling are among the activities encouraged.) The Hoosier Ecologist program was developed for adults, whose participants often have provided considerable aid to the overworked naturalists in peak times. These and other patch programs all involved service, giving visitors opportunities to contribute to their parks. (The patch programs ended in 2007 but were replaced by Hoosier Quest, a comprehensive multi-level program of education and service.) In the late 1970s the Division began to offer to the public structured weekend getaways with the naturalists and other experts giving presentations that focused on specific nature themes. Held at the inns during the winter months, the getaways also were intended to encourage people to come to the parks during the off season. The weekends proved extremely popular but budget constraints resulted in their being discontinued.[19]

In the Division's central office, a new position (since discontinued) of Cultural Arts and Recreation Specialist was created in 1978, originally under the auspices of YACC. Cultural arts programs began modestly enough, with a touring singing group, a drama troupe at Spring Mill, and "Theater in the Woods" at McCormick's Creek. Over the years the program has brought music and other performance groups to parks and given opportunities for Indiana performers to gain a wide audience. Growing budget constraints forced discontinuation of most performance programs in 2002, but some troupers elected to continue to perform on a volunteer basis.[20] Such entertainment may appear far removed from the original mission of the parks, but as early as the 1920s a few of them offered band concerts, and the nature guides of the late 1930s and 1940s were expected to provide light entertainment in addition to their more educational talks and hikes.

Under the Cultural Arts program, the Division began a state parks photography contest in 1980, held annually for several years. Although those competitions were discontinued, the venerable *Outdoor Indiana* magazine holds photo contests frequently. With the help of grants from arts or humanities agencies, some of the parks undertook folk arts projects. Taking a cue from the naturalists, the first Cultural Arts weekend getaway, "A Gathering of Friends," was held at Spring Mill in spring 1982 and featured craftspersons and folk artists. In the summer of 1987, the outdoor drama *Young Abe Lincoln*, under the auspices of the University of Southern Indiana in Evansville, premiered at Lincoln State Park

47

in its new 1500-seat covered amphitheater. A few years later, a second musical production, *Big River*, based on *Huckleberry Finn*, was offered in repertory with the Lincoln play. Every three years another musical production was chosen to alternate with the venerable *Young Abe Lincoln*, until the performances stopped in 2005. (In honor of Lincoln's two hundredth birthday, a brand new production combining live performance with multi-media debuted in June 2009.) From Lieber's time through the present, state parks have always sought to be family-oriented. But the ideal of self-directed activity in the parks was clearly struggling with the growing variety of structured entertainment offered.

Illinois native William C. Walters (b. 1942), formerly head of the Division of Outdoor Recreation, took over the Division of State Parks in 1977 and was largely responsible for expanding the naturalist programs and adding cultural arts and interpretation into the mix. Under his tenure Harmonie and Potato Creek state recreation areas were rededicated as state parks, and the new Summit Lake State

Summit Lake's wetland provides wonderful opportunities for bird watching.   *photo by GJ Greiff*

Park came into the system. But financial challenges loomed on the horizon. In the 1980s budget cuts began a shift in priorities from building and expansion of the properties to more emphasis on maintenance and rehabilitation. By the middle of the decade Indiana's allotment from the federal Land and Water Conservation Fund had so dwindled that no more money was available to the state parks from that source. The General Assembly provided some additional funds, and bonding authority allowed for some improvements in state park inns and nature centers. Still, without the federal funds to ease the financial strain, some maintenance was deferred and staff reduced, and ultimately many seasonal positions were eliminated, including naturalists. Yet people continued to pour into the parks in ever greater numbers. Some new user fees appeared and older ones increased, a method of last resort when dealing with public lands.[21] In 1989 William Walters left to take a position with the National Park Service. Wisconsin-born Gerald J. Pagac (b.1946), who had replaced him as head of the Division of Outdoor Recreation, took over, first as acting, then as the official Director of the Division of State Parks. Shortly thereafter, DNR moved into its new offices in the Indiana Government Center South, and the challenge to stretch a too-thin budget to meet the demands of an ever-growing number of park visitors continued in the 1990s.

 NOTES

1. "DNR Report," 1985, 19.

2. Interview, Foltz. See Frank Weirich, "New Agency Takes Over," *Indianapolis Times*, 18 July 1965; *Master Plan 1978+*, plan prepared by Division of Outdoor Recreation, Indiana Department of Natural Resources, Indianapolis, 1978, 8-13. See also Favinger, "Environmental Era," 25.

3. See *Master Plan 1978+*, 7, 9; Ralph Kramer, "Our State Parks in Crisis: System Suffered as State Slept," *Indianapolis News*, 7 March 1966; "DNR Report," 1970, 45; see also Favinger, "Time of Progress," 36; telephone interview, Pagac, 7 May 2003.

4. Overall planning for state parks is included in that division's State Comprehensive Outdoor Recreational Plan (SCORP), instituted in 1965 with updates at regular intervals.

5. See "DNR Reports," 1965, 1; 1968, 1; "Upstate Park Land Buying to Start Soon," *Indianapolis Star*, 23 March 1968. See also Hasenstab, "Conservation Awakening," 28; Favinger, "Environmental Era," 26.

See later chapters on Harmonie and Potato Creek for further information on the acquisition and development of these properties.

6. The exception was Bass Lake State Beach, which had been administered through nearby Tippecanoe River State Park from 1971 until 2002, when it was turned over to Starke County.

7. "DNR Report," 1968, 1. See also "DNR Reports," 1965, 30; 1979, 134, 138. An executive decision effective in 1996 reunited the two divisions administratively, but the properties are still managed under different policies.

8. In 2004 Wyandotte Woods SRA was renamed O'Bannon Woods State Park and transferred to the Division of State Parks and Reservoirs.

9. It continued to appear well into the 1990s on some, such as the trail map for Pokagon State Park dated November 1994.

10. See "DNR Reports," 1967, 25; 1969, 43; 1970, 1, 44-45. Also, *Master Plan 1978+*, 12.

11. See "DNR Reports," 1970, 1, 48; 1972, 78; Hasenstab, Interview, 2 March 1993.

12. Author's fieldwork, 1990-91, 1995-96. See "DNR Report," 1965, 26.

13. Information on Green Thumb activities gleaned from "DNR Reports," 1968-1985, passim; Telephone interview, Pagac, 5 May 2003.

14. Author's fieldwork, 1990-1991; see Diane Ledger et al., *The Young Adult Conservation Corps and Youth Conservation Corps in Indiana, 1974-1982*. (Indianapolis: Indiana Department of Natural Resources, 1982).

15. See "DNR Report," 1968, 4; 1969, 1; "Indiana State Parks System Plan," 20; *Indiana Recreation Guide 95*, 32.

16. See "DNR Report," 1977, 131. Hasenstab, telephone interview, 23 May 1995; Hasenstab, "Conservation Awakening," 30.

17. "DNR Report," 1972, 79.

18. "DNR Report," 1971, 71.

19. See "DNR Reports," 1971, 71; 1973, 84; 1974, 105, 115; 1977, 131-132; 1979, 152. Author's numerous discussions and fieldwork with longtime naturalists James P. Eagleman, Brown County State Park; Fred J. Wooley, Pokagon State Park, and Richard Davis, Clifty Falls State Park. Author's conversation with John Bergman, Assistant Director, Division of State Parks and Reservoirs, and Ginger Murphy, State Coordinator, Division of State Parks and Reservoirs, 9 October 2008.

20. See "DNR Reports," 1979, 135-136, 157; 1980, 164; George McLaren, "Red Ink, Greenspace," *Indianapolis Star* 30 July 2002.

21. See "DNR Reports," 1981, 1; 1983, 196-197; 1984, 215-216; 1985, 18-19; Susan Hanafee, "State Parks in Bad Shape, Future Gloomy, Study Says," *Indianapolis Star*, 4 June 1989; http// www.rpts.tamu.edu/Pugsley/Walters.htm.

A QUESTION OF BALANCE: TODAY'S STATE PARKS

"When the congestion of an ever-increasing population. . .
has changed everything but these primitive places, our state parks
will be one of the most priceless possessions of our people."[1]

Except for the degree of their severity, few problems that face parks today were unknown or entirely unanticipated. From the unexpectedly large crowds that sought solace at the barely developed Turkey Run and McCormick's Creek after World War I, to the unhappy campers in the 1950s who could not find a spot to pitch a tent, to today's would-be picnickers at Indiana Dunes who are turned away from the overstuffed park at nine in the morning, Hoosiers have loved their parks to the point of destruction. A major evaluative study of the state park system in 1989 had summed up the problem as "too many people at the wrong time or at the wrong place." The most popular parks are, of course, the ones most in need of respite. Trails have been trampled into hardened lanes; ground beneath picnic areas and campgrounds has become so packed that water rolls off and puddles as if it were concrete. Several parks have erected wooden walks that may appear intrusive but help save the soil in fragile areas. Yet the public at times seems scarcely aware that its play—sometimes just by the sheer volume of it—threatens a park's natural and built environment, and that steps taken to preserve the park could interfere with their ideas of recreation. It seems that people have always wanted "both fun and flora" in their parks, and the balance, teetering under the best of circumstances, grows ever more precarious.[2]

And the flora have been severely threatened by a problem that several of the state parks encountered by the 1990s, which would have been inconceivable in the early years of Indiana parks: too many deer. They tend to gobble up new growth on the forest floor and all tree branches within their quite-high reach. Today's overpopulation hearkens back to the release in Indiana of white-tail deer beginning in the late 1930s, a time when the only such creatures in the state parks were enclosed in pens. The reintroduction of once-common native animals that have disappeared from the wild has become an accepted conservation practice in some cases. Wild turkeys were brought back to Indiana in the 1980s, for example, where they have become a very visible presence in several state parks, and river otters released in the 1990s are thriving. (More controversial are the experiments with re-introducing wolves in the West, and, closer to home, in Kentucky.) Indiana's deer problem might have been foreseen; as early as the 1910s there was a problem

By the 1980s, overpopulation of deer caused the hungry animals to be too trusting and once-rare daytime sightings were commonplace.   *photo by GJ Greiff*

of too many deer in the area north of the Grand Canyon, and they were dying because of predator eradication and too little food. Conservationist Aldo Leopold spoke of deer overpopulation in Wisconsin in the 1930s, but few wanted to listen; the deer being reintroduced in Indiana around that time were ultimately meant to be hunted, after all. (Limited hunting of deer began in the 1950s.) Lack of predators and too little food, combined with modern suburban sprawl that wrought a dramatic loss of habitat, made the problem even worse today. Animal rights protesters, a phenomenon that grew out of the raised environmental consciousness of the 1960s, often attempted to block efforts to deal with the deer.[3]

Regardless of one's feelings about animal rights, the fact remains that deer herds had overrun several of Indiana's state parks and severely damaged their forests and fields, grazing the understory to the ground and destroying saplings—and consequently, the habitats of other creatures. Once the glimpse of a flashing white tail dashing off through the woods was a rare thrill one might hope for; there is little soul-stirring in the unnatural sight of a malnourished deer herd milling around an open field at high noon, which had become a common sight in Brown County. In the early 1990s, after numerous public hearings and considering several alternatives, DNR instigated a controversial program of limited and controlled hunting on the park properties most affected. The efforts have proven generally successful, and while there are still some protests from animal rights activists, they have become far less vociferous. Invasive flora have become as great a problem as the deer had been; indeed, marauding plants such as garlic mustard were able to get a toehold in part because the deer had consumed the native plants, leaving forest floors bare. Eradication of these unwanted species has been incorporated into park education programs and volunteer efforts.[4]

Even more controversial was the decision in 2006 to allow handguns into state parks where they had always been banned; now people who have a personal protection permit may carry their handguns into the parks. Despite considerable protest from concerned citizens and numerous editorialists, a substantial number of Hoosiers supported removing the ban, and the policy remains in place today.[5]

All indications are that a substantial portion of the people of Indiana will continue to seek play or peace in their state parks, and so attention had turned again in the late 1980s to the acquisition of new land for more parks. Studies and plans had long targeted the Lafayette area as lacking a state park sufficiently

near. In the 1970s a proposal to dam Wildcat Creek and create a recreational area on what would have been called Lafayette Lake died in the Legislature. Another site chosen by DNR a few years later near the town of Colburn was shot down by citizen opposition. In 1989, DNR finally selected an unlikely tract marred by railroad tracks, a power line and an interstate just northeast of Lafayette.[6] Admittedly, what ultimately became Prophetstown State Park was far from a beauty

Barn under construction for the 1920s living history farm at Prophetstown. *photo by GJ Greiff* spot, but many people gazing upon the stripmined desolation of the future Shakamak State Park in 1929 must have felt similar dismay. Located on about three hundred acres within the new state park is a museum complex established by a regional not-for-profit organization—an example of one of the more recent public-private partnerships that has arisen since money has been so tight.

A completely different sort of site, unquestionably worthy of being preserved but almost completely lacking in recreational facilities, came into the state park system in the early 1990s through a cooperative agreement among several government agencies and a not-for-profit organization. Long noted for its geological and historical significance, the Falls of the Ohio, along with two adjacent islands, had become a National Wildlife Conservation Area in 1982, even though it was in the midst of a large urban area and had been environmentally abused for decades. Clearly worth saving, an agreement was reached that established a small state park that encompassed a large portion of the Devonian Era fossil beds, the homesite of pre-state Indiana's greatest hero, George Rogers Clark, and a superb interpretive center, funded through bonds sold by the city of Clarksville. Unlike any other Indiana park, and unlikely ever to reach even a hundred acres in area, Falls of the Ohio State Park was dedicated in 1994.[7]

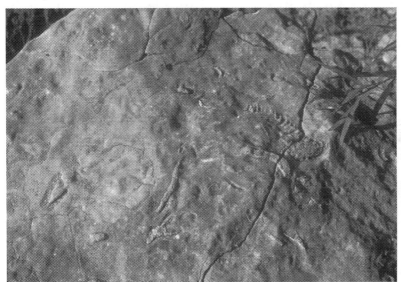

The eye falls upon fossils everywhere at Falls of the Ohio.

photo by GJ Greiff

The closing of military installations offered the Division of State Parks unanticipated new opportunities to acquire highly desirable forested land. The Army shut down the World War II-era ammunition plant at Charlestown in the 1980s; the Division acquired about 850 acres in 1994 and later acquired over a thousand more at the site's north end. Much of the parcel, part of which had previously been an amusement park, is heavily wooded and rocky with deep ravines and steep bluffs overlooking the Ohio River. Charlestown is a state park in the traditional mode, its forbidding topography as much a factor as policy —and budget—in the decision to develop it slowly. Its chief delights are picnicking, hiking, fishing and camping. The closing of Fort Benjamin Harrison finally presented the Indianapolis metropolitan area with a nearly ready park practically on its doorstep. While its trails through lovely woodlands, already well-known to local birdwatchers and nature lovers, suggest a state park of which Richard Lieber would approve, he—and others—might recoil at the existing golf course, formerly part of the army base, included on the property.[8] Charlestown and Fort Harrison state parks both formally opened in October 1996.

Budget problems that surfaced in the 1980s grew to alarming proportions in the next decade and into the new millennium, resulting in constant efforts to cut back spending, which threatened the maintenance and preservation of increasingly overused facilities. At first, in the early 1990s, there were reductions in seasonal workers, from naturalists to laborers, all of which meant fewer services to the public. Cutbacks in hiring lifeguards, for example, meant that swimming hours were lessened or that part of a beach might be closed. Some of the hikes, sing-alongs, and other such participatory programs involving naturalists that many park visitors had come to expect had to be curtailed. Fewer

The popular amusement park at Rose Island, site of Charlestown State Park, was destroyed in the Flood of 1937.

Division of State Parks archives

maintenance workers meant grassy areas were mowed less often—or not at all—and that trash cans were not being emptied as quickly. Indeed, in 1994, the Department introduced a controversial policy of having day visitors to the parks carry out their own trash, a mostly successful program which remains in effect today.[9]

Despite these problems foreshadowing more difficulties down the road, the Natural Resources Commission, urged on by Governor Evan Bayh, approved curtailment of a number of park fees in 1995, eliminating many small rental fees entirely and reducing several others. But in less than two years, a study was undertaken as to whether the fees needed to be reinstated or even raised. Some were, such as overnight rates in the inns, and in 2002, entrance and camping fees took a major jump upwards, even as seasonal employees continued to be reduced.[10] In the same year that it approved fee reductions, the Natural Resources Commission, motivated primarily by financial concerns, also authorized a merger between the Division of State Parks and the Division of Reservoir Management, effective 1 February 1996. In addition, some lands adjacent to each other or in close proximity were placed under the same manager, essentially uniting some properties that formerly were administered by separate divisions. While these actions gave the appearance of more efficient government through streamlining and the elimination of several mid-level managers, the mergers created local administrative headaches since the combined properties were still operated under different sets of rules.[11]

Since state parks are so beloved (albeit often to their detriment in overuse), when the public began to notice there were problems with cleanup and other staffing shortages, people began to offer help. While volunteer organizations had been long established in some other states, Indiana, apart from its Park Patch Program that encouraged good stewardship, did not have any framework established to accept such help. As Director Gerald J. Pagac noted in 1992, however, "for all that the volunteers do, it is not quite the same as being able to count on somebody being there like an employee." Still, over the next decade and more, volunteers have proven to be of tremendous value in keeping the parks running smoothly. Formal guidelines have been set up for volunteers, whether individuals, families, or groups, and a system of awards established for levels of service. Some of the established parks rather quickly found themselves in the 1990s with "Friends of" groups; a statewide group was clearly the next step, and momentum is growing toward that end. The fitness movement of recent years created a clamor for mountain bike trails, which have been constructed in several of the parks. Bicyclists' organizations such as the Hoosier Mountain Bike Association have helped greatly in planning and building the trails. And in 2007, the Division of State Parks and Reservoirs unveiled Hoosier Quest, a comprehensive multi-level program of education and service that expanded upon and replaced the former park patch program.[12]

The continuing budget crunch, of course, also meant that many plans had to be cut back, postponed, or canceled entirely. Periodically much is made of the fact that there has not been an inn built at a state park since the one at Spring Mill in 1939, although there have been numerous expansions and remodelings of extant buildings. As it happened, Fort Harrison came into the system with some structures that were able to be adapted for a limited number of overnight accommodations. But the economic climate has been far too inclement to consider such a tremendous expenditure as the construction of new inns. The idea might be justified only if a new inn would be likely to pull its weight throughout the entire year by attracting conferences. The ever-expanding event business has indeed proven a boon to most of the existing park inns, and remodeling projects in recent years have included increased facilities to encourage planners to use state park inns for off-season conferences.[13]

Spring Mill Inn shortly after construction in the late 1930s.

collection of Tom Hohman

The Division's financial woes would certainly have suggested that the acquisition of new property was a distant dream, but in 2004 Indiana's twenty-fourth state park entered the system with virtually the flick of a pen. The previous fall, Governor Frank O'Bannon, a native of Harrison County, suffered a stroke and died in office. His Lieutenant Governor and successor Joe Kernan renamed the former Wyandotte Woods SRA, situated in the midst of the Harrison-Crawford State Forest that Governor O'Bannon and his family had loved so well. O'Bannon Woods State Park honored three generations of the family, and the property, long used by the public already, moved from the Division of State Forests to the Division of State Parks. Its rugged topography and lovely views of the Ohio River fit the traditional criteria of what a state park should be, one of which Richard Lieber would have heartily approved.

With a new administration in 2005 came sweeping changes almost akin to those that led to Richard Lieber's resignation in 1933. Governor Mitch Daniels installed Kyle Hupfer as the new DNR director, a position which historically has been a political appointment. Those who ran the myriad of divisions within the department, however, normally were not subject to the whims of changing parties. But with the governor's blessing, Hupfer proceeded to replace a large number of department heads, including Gerald Pagac, who had ably directed the Division of State Parks since 1989. For decades the director's position had been filled with qualified professionals with education and/or experience in conservation or recreation. Pagac's replacement, Hoosier-born Daniel W. Bortner (b.1964), a human resources specialist, does not have that background, but he has demonstrated a willingness to collaborate with those who have greater experience in the parks. Bortner strongly believes in Richard Lieber's mission, despite how distorted it has become over nearly a century.[14]

Lieber was a pragmatist, and while he held fast to his own ideas of what belonged in a state park and what people should seek there, he realized, no doubt with a sigh, that what soothes one person's soul gives no peace to another. Hoosiers love their parks, but express that affection in myriad ways. Thus, within limits that have been severely stretched for close to a century, today's parks must accommodate the needs of the many. However they use them, perhaps in their hearts most people believe as Lieber, that parks are

> the crowning glory of our land; rich storehouses of memories and reveries; guides and counsels to the weary and faltering in spirit; bearers of wonderful tales to him who will listen; a solace to the aged and an inspiration to the young.[15]

 NOTES

1. Richard Lieber, speech made 10 October 1928, quoted in *Indiana 2001 Recreation Guide*.

2. Quotations, respectively from *DNR Sunset Review*, study by Office of Fiscal and Management Analysis, 1989 (on file at the Division of State Park, and Susan Hanafee, "State Parks Ready for a New Season Under a New Chief," *Indianapolis Star*, 29 April 1990. See *Ibid*; Interview, Pagac; Interview, Ralston and Costello; Hanafee, "State Parks in Bad Shape, Future Gloomy, Study Says," *Indianapolis Star*, 4 June 1989.

3. See Dunlap, *Saving America's Wildlife*, especially 65-70; Flader, *Thinking Like a Mountain*, especially chapter 5, "Too Many Deer;" Curt Meine, *Aldo Leopold: His Life and Work* (Madison: University of Wisconsin Press, 1988), 457-458, 462-464, 467-469, 487-489 *et al.*; Greiff, "New Deal Work Projects on Indiana State Lands"; author's fieldwork, 1991-1992, and discussions with park naturalists Eagleman and Wooley.

4. Author's fieldwork, 1991-1992, and discussions with park naturalists Eagleman and Wooley. Press coverage of the state park deer hunts has been extensive; see, for example, Kyle Niederpruem, "Brown County Herd Gets Reprieve," *Indianapolis Star*, 19 April 1993; "Deer Herd Grows at State Park," *Indianapolis News*, 16 December 1994; Michele McNeil, "Deer Hunting Sought for Parks," *Indianapolis Star*, 19 January 1995; Skip Hess, "Controlled Hunts Needed," *Indianapolis News*, 8 September 1995. See also *Deer Management and Ecosystem Restoration in Indiana State Parks*, brochure published by DNR, n.d.

5. See, for example, Will Higgins, "Pack a Picnic—Or a Gun," *Indianapolis Star*, 22 September 2006; "Readers Take Sides Over Guns in Parks," *Indianapolis Star*, 26 September 2006; Matthew Tully, "Weapons at Parks? Let's Tell 'Em to Take a Hike," *Indianapolis Star*, 27 September 2006.

6. See Jeanne Norberg, "Senate Moves to Create Midstate Park," Lafayette Journal and Courier, 5 February 1982; "Tippecanoe Site of New Park," Indianapolis News, 12 November 1982; Jeff Swiatek, "Proposed Park Site is Short of Trees, Long on Controversy," Indianapolis Star, 10 September 1989.

7. "Falls of the Ohio Center Opens," *Indianapolis News*, 25 January 1994; Tom Chiat, "Back from Extinction," *Indianapolis Star*, 13 March 1994.

8. Welton W. Harris II, "Plans for Fort Park to Be Discussed," *Indianapolis News* 11 November 1993; "New State Parks Would Need Money," *Indianapolis News*, 27 March 1995. David Griffith, Division of State Parks Planning Section, telephone interview, 15 June 1995.

9. Susan Hanafee, "State Parks Trim Work Force by 111," *Indianapolis Star*, 8 May 1992; "State Park Patrons Take to New Carry-Out Policy on Trash," *Indianapolis News*, 9 June 1994.

10. "Park fee Reductions, DNR Merger Approved," *South Bend Tribune*, 2 December 1995; Barb Albert, "Park Fees May Be Changed, " *Indianapolis Star*, 22 March 1997; Kyle Niederpruem, "Park Inns Expected to Raise Their Rates," *Indianapolis Star*, 25 April 1997; Don Porter, "State Parks Wrestle with Money Issues," *South Bend Tribune*, 14 April 2002; "Parks Raise Fees, Cut Costs to Make Budget," *South Bend Tribune*, 17 May 2002; George McLaren, "Happy Campers? Not After the State's Latest Fee Increases," *Indianapolis Star*, 19 July 2002; McLaren, "Red Ink, Greenspace," *Star*, 30 July 2002.

11. Pagac, Interview with author, 4 March 2003; "Park fee Reductions, DNR Merger Approved," *South Bend Tribune*, 2 December 1995.

12. Pagac quoted in Hanafee, "State Parks Trim Work Force," 8 May 1992; Porter, "State Parks Wrestle," 14 April 2002; *Volunteer Indiana State Parks and Reservoirs*. Brochure distributed by DNR, 2003; Pagac, Interview, 4 March 2003; author's conversation with John Bergman, Assistant Director, Division of State Parks and Reservoirs, and Ginger Murphy, State Coordinator, Division of State Parks and Reservoirs, 9 October 2008.

13. Pagac, Interview, 4 March 2003.

14. Pagac, letter to author, 9 October 2008; author's interview with Daniel W. Bortner, Director of State Parks and Reservoirs, State of Indiana Department of Natural Resources, 20 May 2008.

15. Lieber, *America's Natural Wealth*, 194.

McCORMICK'S CREEK STATE PARK
(Established 1916)

The limestone canyons and ravines of McCormick's Creek, named for the first white settler who owned the property, were once hunting grounds for native Americans of the Miami tribe. Little in the way of agricultural development penetrated the heavily wooded slopes, although a few mills briefly flourished along the creek and White River, and in the 1880s a limestone quarry provided material for Indiana's statehouse. But the area remained largely undisturbed, a lovely and peaceful haven. In 1888 Dr. Frederick Denkewalter purchased a sizable tract along the creek in order to open a recuperative sanitarium and continued to add acreage to his property over the next several years. The sanitarium's main building, which later served as the park's first hotel, stood on the site of today's Canyon Inn; the original foundations remain part of the present structure. After Denkewalter's death in 1914, his estate was offered for auction. An area long familiar to geologists and nature lovers as a destination of high scenic beauty, McCormick's Creek seemed ideally suited for a state park. After approaching the State Park Committee, citizens of Owen County raised funds for the purchase, which the state matched.[1]

McCormick's Creek Canyon State Park ("Canyon" was later dropped from the name) was Indiana's first, established in 1916 even before the Indiana Department of Conservation was created. Within a few years, the sanitarium was remodeled into a park inn, some picnic areas established, and a few trails built. A small dam across McCormick's Creek below the falls provided a lovely pool for frolicking in the water, but it was some distance from the inn. The park became very popular and attendance increased by leaps and bounds each year. In response, the Department of Conservation in the late 1920s saw to the construction of a proper swimming pool and

This abandoned quarry is one of the interesting sights along McCormick's Creek.

photo by GJ Greiff

57

The pool was replaced by a newer one connected to the Inn; it is now a recreation center.

Division of State Parks archives

bath house (rehabilitated into today's recreation center) near the inn. It was the first pool to be built in a state park, and for nearly twenty years one of only two in the system. During the 1920s, on land that had been a small farm, the Division of Forestry set up plots of experimental tree plantings in the area of the present campground. By the early 1930s McCormick's Creek was one of two state parks offering group camping facilities geared toward youth organizations. With the continuously growing usage of the park, it was clear that more of the property needed to be made accessible to visitors.[2]

The coming of Franklin Roosevelt's New Deal and the Civilian Conservation Corps was timely. CCC Camp SP-4 was established with Company 589 occupying it from November 1933 until July 1935, which enabled McCormick's Creek to undertake an ambitious and much-needed new development program. Along with some reforestation, landscaping, and additional road and trail building, the CCC boys worked on the construction of numerous outdoor recreational buildings and the supporting infrastructure, and indeed, shaped much of the park as we know it today. The CCC built an unusually fine stone arch bridge across McCormick's Creek above the falls, thus making the area known as Beech Grove (part of the present campground) accessible to park visitors by way of a scenic road that essentially paralleled the creek past Echo Canyon and then veered northward. The area above Echo Canyon, too, could now be developed as a picnic area. The boys completed the attractive gatehouse at the park entrance shortly before the camp closed and Company 589 relocated to a new camp near Lagro in Wabash County.[3] Both the stone arch bridge and the gatehouse and entrance are listed in the National Register of Historic Places.

After the CCC camp was abandoned in 1935, a group of WPA workers cleared the site, leaving only the recreation hall standing in place. In response to public demand, the WPA remodeled the building for use as a nature museum—the first in any Indiana state park. The museum opened in 1936, housing displays, photographs, and live animals and fish; it also served as a center for lectures explaining various aspects of the natural world and as a takeoff point for nature hikes. The building is listed in the National Register of Historic Places. WPA workers also constructed an amphitheater, refurbished in 2007, on a hillside adjacent to two of the group camps and not far from the hotel.[4]

In 1940 another group of CCC workers, who trucked over daily from Brown County, undertook a new round of development that included the Redbud Shelter. But World War II intervened before all the intended construction could be completed. After the war, the previously planned group of family housekeeping cabins were among the first projects park employees tackled, using the CCC blueprints.[5]

McCormick's Creek was the only park ever to offer three group camps; ultimately, it had six, which were always filled to capacity each summer until usage began to wane in the 1970s. Two camps remain but they are often empty, particularly during the week, although usage seems to be on the rise again. The building of a new bridge upstream from the CCC's stone arch span provided access to land acquired in the 1970s that enlarged the visitor capacity of McCormick's Creek and provided space to build both a new nature center and a public swimming pool without intruding upon the older parts of the park.[6] McCormick's Creek State Park is among the most highly developed with its

The stone arch bridge constructed by the CCC is listed in the National Register of Historic Places.

photo by GJ Greiff

recreation center, tennis courts and modern swimming pool, and is a popular site for conferences. But it still offers vast tracts of beautiful natural scenery with ample opportunity for encounters with nature. There is even a much-loved small cave, located in one of the parks two nature preserves. The wooded bluffs, rocky canyons, and sun-dappled glens beckon the hiker in search of nature's solace, especially so in spring and fall.

 NOTES

1. See Chas. [sic] G. Sauers, *McCormick's Creek Canyon State Park: A History and Description* (Indianapolis: The Department of Conservation: State of Indiana, 1923); Edward Barrett, *Indiana Department of Geology and Natural Resources 41st Annual Report, 1916* (Fort Wayne: Fort Wayne Printing Company, 1917).

2. Information on park development found throughout "Conservation Reports," 1919-1930, passim.

3. Information on the work of the CCC in McCormick's Creek found in "Conservation Reports," 1934-1935, passim; and RG35, E-115 "Camp Inspection Reports," Box 71, NA. See Greiff, "New Deal Resources in Present Indiana State Parks," 1991. Field survey on file at DHPA.

4. *Ibid.*; RG79, E-44 "Records Concerning WPA Projects," Box 4, NA; R4269, Box 40, "State Parks: Shakamak/Winamac," Folder, "McCormick's Creek, WPA 9284," SA. See *Outdoor Indiana* 3 (September 1936), 19-25.

5. Blueprints, Family Housekeeping Cabins," ECW McCormick's Creek State Park, 1939-1940, on file at McCormick's Creek. See "Conservation Reports," 1948, 809; 1949, 269.

6. Developments noted in "DNR Reports," 1965, 26; 1971, 68.

TURKEY RUN STATE PARK
(Established 1916)

What should have been Indiana's first state park was denied that honor because of the larger pocketbook of the Hoosier Veneer Company, which outbid the State Park Committee in the spring of 1916 to acquire the estate of the eccentric John Lusk. Known to many as Bloomingdale Glens, the rugged land straddling Sugar Creek in northern Parke County was heavily forested with a variety of massive trees, which the lumber company had planned to harvest. But public outcry, mobilized by the likes of writer Juliet V. Strauss and Richard Lieber, persuaded the new owners to sell the property to the state at a tidy profit of $10,000. Like his father, Captain Salmon Lusk, who had settled on the land in the 1820s, John Lusk had cherished his mighty trees. He gladly shared their beauty with visitors to the camping resort he maintained on the property, but had steadfastly refused to sell even a small parcel to lumber interests. The younger Lusk had lived a hermit's life in the substantial brick house his father had built in 1841 above his mill on the north side of the Narrows of Sugar Creek. Foundation remnants of the mill are all that remain today, but the Lusk home, listed in the National Register of Historic Places and restored in 1982, still stands proudly (and is open for tours in season). Turkey Run became Indiana's second state park in late 1916. The name Turkey Run, incidentally, refers to the great flocks of wild turkeys that once sought shelter within the stream's canyon walls.[1]

When acquired by the state, the property had an inn left over from the younger Lusk's resort camp to provide food service, but the only overnight accommodations were canvas tents, equipped with cots, erected on wooden platforms. The entrance road was west of the stream for which the park is named and led straight to the inn via a concrete vehicular bridge built in 1914 over Turkey Hollow. Today, sections of that road and the bridge are part of a trail, reminding hikers that automobiles once crossed

Once part of a county road, this bridge today serves Trail 11.

photo by GJ Greiff

here. Richard Lieber was alarmed by another span on the property, the "frail hanging bridge" over Sugar Creek, so he immediately had a cable suspension bridge constructed to replace it.[2]

After World War I, park employees razed the old inn and built a new hotel, which proved its "utter incapacity" within its first year. Hordes of people descending upon Turkey Run had to be turned away. Some found accommodations in farmhouses in the vicinity, and primitive camping was available. The park immediately added five bungalow cottages next to the inn, which helped only a little. Public demand was relentless. The open cars of the day gave merit to repeated requests for some sort of shelter, so an open-sided garage was built nearby. In 1922 the Department responded to the need for overnight facilities with a two-story brick annex, soon enlarged, just south of the earlier hotel building. A few years later, amenities for inn patrons included tennis courts and a children's playground, which Lieber reluctantly permitted because "people who come to stay more than a day should be provided for." More in keeping with his notion of a state park was the nature guide service on weekends that Turkey Run was the first to offer. During the 1920s the park added more land, mostly north across Sugar Creek, including Rocky Hollow, today a nature preserve.[3]

Richard Lieber always considered the establishment of state parks as preserving history, and for a time he envisioned a collection of pioneer structures at Turkey Run to educate visitors about early nineteenth century life. Beginning with a cabin he had moved onto the property shortly after the park was acquired, Lieber added a log church in 1923, taken from a site about five miles away.[4] But a few years later a new property in Lawrence County that included a three-story mill and some surviving dwellings seemed a more suitable place to pursue this idea, which evolved into the village at Spring Mill State Park. The cabin at Turkey Run served as a museum for many years, housing mostly pioneer implements, and today houses exhibits about Lieber. It is listed in the National Register of Historic Places. The log church in its wooded clifftop setting holds Sunday services in the warm months.

Two sculptures at Turkey Run commemorate persons especially significant in the history of the state park. *Subjugation*, a bronze sculpture of a classical female figure raising a chalice above several allegorical creatures, which symbolized the triumph of the spiritual over the material, was dedicated in 1922. The statue honored nationally syndicated columnist Juliet Strauss (1863-1918) of Rockville, "the Country Contributor" who had worked so hard to save Turkey Run. The Women's Press Club of Indiana commissioned the well known Indianapolis sculptor Myra Reynolds Richards for the work. Although originally placed near the inn, it was moved and stood for over forty years within Turkey Hollow. In the early 1990s it was refurbished and placed on a new base toward the rear of the inn.[5]

The Lieber Monument not long after its dedication.

photo by GJ Greiff

Not far from the old log church is a bronze bust of Richard Lieber by E. H. Daniels, commissioned by the Nature Study Club. Unveiled in 1932, the last year of Lieber's directorship, the sculpture now marks his grave, for the ashes of "the Father of Indiana State Parks" rest below. Lieber died in 1944; ironically, he is said to have remarked at the monument's dedication twelve years earlier that he felt "like a corpse hearing his eulogy."[6]

The Depression had slowed further development at Turkey Run but in 1933 a Civil Works Administration (CWA) project employed men from the region to work on service roads and to quarry stone. In 1934 CCC Company 1543, comprised of veterans, transferred from Lincoln State Park and established Camp SP-8 at Turkey Run. In a little over a year they completed a gatehouse and landscaping on the new main entrance, a new campground (now the Canyon Picnic Area) with modern improvements, and three shelter houses. The CCC camp was discontinued in the fall of 1935, but another New Deal program entered the picture for the next two years. WPA workers built trails, a log shelter house, dozens of picnic tables, thirty ovens, and several comfort stations. The CCC camp reopened in 1938 with a new contingency of young men, Company 2580. They constructed a service building of stone and the stone-and-timber saddle barn. The CCC boys completed the five overnight cabins adjacent to the inn before the camp was abandoned in March 1942. The new commissary building they were working on was three-quarters done, which park employees were able to finish by the following year.[7] The building, much remodeled, today houses the park's nature center, dedicated in 1986.

Traffic on the county road that formed the east boundary of Turkey Run traveled over the Narrows of Sugar Creek through a picturesque covered bridge built in 1882—not surprising in Parke County, which not unjustly calls itself the "Covered Bridge Capital of the World." In the late 1950s the county constructed a new concrete bridge just east of the old one and west of the Lusk Mill site, which effectively placed the covered bridge—today listed in the National Register of Historic Places —in the park. Otherwise, little

The Lusk Home & Narrows Bridge at Turkey Run, 1940s
Division of State Parks archives

changed at Turkey Run in the 1950s and 1960s, except greater crowds and louder clamors for campsites. The opening of Shades State Park only ten miles away in 1947 perhaps helped ease the strain.

In the early 1970s Turkey Run established a youth tent camp area on land originally occupied by the privately owned Ravina Lodge, which the park razed when it acquired that property. To the west was built a much-needed large new campground on relatively treeless land. The idea was to preserve the forest areas, for a heavily used campground takes its toll on the forest floor, its root systems, and its drainage. In the park's early years, people swam in Sugar Creek, still a delightful (but forbidden) temptation for many on simmering summer days. But in 1975 a swimming pool, used extensively by the local population, was added to Turkey Run's amenities. In 2008 the park completed a new amphitheater for outdoor programming.[8]

The streams and gorges of Turkey Run still call to those who seek nature's true spirit. Remarkably cool within, the canyons brim with discoveries at every turn, from a sluggish snake coiled on the sand to a tenacious clump of flowers lit by a sunbeam halfway up the sandstone walls.

Aptly named Sunset Point is a peaceful spot overlooking Sugar Creek.   *photo by GJ Greiff*

 NOTES

1. See "Report of State Park Committee," (1917), 496-497; "Silver Anniversary of State Parks Is Celebrated With Dinner at Turkey Run," *Outdoor Indiana* 9 (January 1942), 13; E. Lieber, *Richard Lieber*, 81-88; Tilden, "Turkey Run State Park," *State Parks: Their Meaning*, 344-349; "DNR Report," 1982, 162. See also Boomhower, *The Country Contributor*.

2. Writer's field surveys, 1990-1995; "Report of State Park Commission," 1918, 542-543.

3. Construction information from "Conservation Reports," 1920-1930, passim. Quotation from 1923, 673.

4. "Report of State Park Commission," 1918, 542; "Conservation Report," 1923, 673.

5. Greiff, 61-006 "Subjugation"/Juliet Strauss Monument, Indiana Save Outdoor Sculpture! (SOS!) survey, on file at Historic Landmarks Foundation of Indiana, 340 West Michigan, Indianapolis IN 46202, hereafter, HLFI. Author's field survey, 27 December 1999.

6. Richard Lieber quoted in E. Lieber, *Richard Lieber*, 131.
Greiff, 61-007, Lieber Monument, SOS! survey, HLFI.

7. RG35, E-115 "Camp Inspection Reports," Box 72, NA; "Conservation Reports," 1934-1942, passim.

8. See "Conservation Report," 1959, 8; DNR Reports," 1974, 114; 1975, 8; Interview, Foltz.

CLIFTY FALLS STATE PARK
(Established 1920)

The area encompassing Clifty Falls near the Ohio River in Jefferson County offered the sort of rough and relatively pristine terrain that Richard Lieber had in mind for the state's new park system. But it was not quite so untouched as it may have appeared. There had been some earlier efforts at farming in the area, although there was little flat land that did not quickly end in a steep drop. In the mid-nineteenth century John Brough, president of the Madison and Indianapolis Railroad Company, had attempted to construct a railroad up and through the forested ridges, but financial difficulties forced him to give up the venture. "Brough's Folly," as the project came to be known, left a legacy of partially completed tunnels, grades, and bridge abutments that are still visible. Remnants form a part of the park's network of trails.[1]

In 1920 Clifty Falls became Indiana's third state park. Through public subscription the citizens of Jefferson County presented an "extremely rugged" area encompassing the Falls as a gift to the Department of Conservation, with matching funds from the state for development. Over the next decade the Department acquired additional adjacent land and renovated an abandoned stone farmhouse high on a bluff overlooking the Ohio into a park inn, then built a new one and used the house as an annex. They erected a shelterhouse at the north end of the park above the Falls and constructed a custodian's cottage, a campground, several foot trails, and a single winding road north to south through the park.[2]

In November 1933, CCC Company 1597 set up and occupied Camp SP-6 at the southern end of the park, northwest of the present nature center. The young men of the CCC began a variety of work projects that shaped much of the park as we know it today. They built new entrance roads and attractive matching gatehouses, completed in 1935, at the north and south ends of the park. Work at the south entrance included an impressive wooden trestle bridge, replaced in the late 1940s, but the CCC's stone arch bridges and smaller culverts are still in place on the main park road. The youthful workers constructed several picnic shelters and fireplace ovens throughout the park, some a little close for comfort to a canyon's edge. These were later demolished, but the Beech Grove Shelter and Clifty Shelter, remodeled from one built in the 1920s, survive. The last building constructed under CCC auspices was the stone and timber saddle barn. (In 1974 a line of tornadoes destroyed most of the horse trails, and the Department renovated the saddle barn into a nature center.)[3]

CCC boys completed this arched bridge in 1936.

photo by GJ Greiff

64

In 1938, the park's master plan fulfilled, the CCC Company vacated Clifty Falls, dismantling the frame buildings of their camp. The site became a campground for park visitors a few years later, but has been long abandoned and left to "naturalize." Clifty Falls offered the first motel accommodations in a state park, in a motor lodge of modern design completed in 1967. Storms in 1974 destroyed the old park inn and badly damaged the new building; the motel was rehabilitated and augmented by considerable new construction. Three decades later major remodeling, demolition of the motel portion, and considerable new construction resulted in the current Clifty Inn and Conference Center.[4]

The acreage of Clifty Falls State Park more than doubled in 1964 with the acquisition of adjoining land to the east that had been part of the Madison State Hospital grounds. As this property had been cultivated farmland, it was an ideal location for various new recreational facilities, such as the swimming pool and a new and larger campground, that would not intrude on the original park's rugged grandeur.[5] Today, trees have obscured most of the views overlooking the Ohio River; perhaps it is just as well, for an ill-placed power plant adjacent to the water mars the sight from several vantage points. But still, the beautiful wooded canyons of Clifty Falls offer among the finest and most vigorous hiking opportunities to be found in any of Indiana's state parks. Little can match the thrill of glimpsing a pair of hawks wheeling high in the brilliant blue summer sky above the canyon.

Built by the CCC as a saddle barn, this building now houses the park's Nature Center.

photo by GJ Greiff

 NOTES

1. Fieldwork and consultations with park naturalist Richard Davis, 1991-1993.
2. Construction information gleaned from "Conservation Reports," 1921-1932, passim.
3. Greiff, "New Deal Resources." "DNR Reports," 1974, 104; 1979, 140.
4. Information gleaned from "Conservation Report," 1938, 896; "DNR Reports," 1966, 24; 1974, 106; 1975, 101.
5. See "Conservation Report," 1964, 11; "DNR Reports," 1968, 5; 1975, 101.

INDIANA DUNES STATE PARK
(Established 1925)

To many of the thousands of Chicagoans and Calumet-area Hoosiers who pour into the park on torrid summer weekends, Indiana Dunes means little more than a nice public beach on Lake Michigan. To Richard Lieber, however, it was "plainly the duty of the State to rescue this land of unsurpassed beauty and protect it for all time to come."[1]

He was not alone. Many before Lieber had discovered the unique wonders of the duneland along Lake Michigan. Its desolate landscape and shifting sands had spared most of the area from encroachment until after the turn of the century. Then in Lake County the frontier town of Gary— for a time as wild as any in the West— sprang up around the new steel mills; related industries saw the possibilities, bulldozed the dunes, mined the sand— and the likelihood of losing one of nature's special places loomed large. Besides the living sand hills, amidst the dunes were swamps, bogs, river bottoms, prairies, each with its unique ecosystem and yet interdependent. W.S. Blatchley, the state geologist, had noted in 1897 that there was no better place in the state "for an extended botanical study of a limited area." Several eminent botanists, notably Henry C. Cowles, spent time in the dunes and published their studies.[2]

In many respects, Chicagoans have always laid some claim to the dunes— and not without reason. Probably the earliest organization to make an effort to preserve some part of Indiana's dunes was the Prairie Club of Chicago, a group of nature lovers and natural scientists who built their "Beach House" high atop a dune north of Tremont, a stop on the South Shore and South Bend Railroad interurban line. Among their members were would-be nymphs, dressed in Grecian mode *a la* Isadora Duncan, dancing in the dunes, as surviving photographs from the 1910s attest. The dunes were easily accessible from Chicago by interurban, and the South

Lake Michigan seems to go wild with joy in September.

photo by GJ Greiff

Shore actively promoted visits to the area. Many individuals came to the dunes to marvel; such folk produced books of a more esthetic nature than those of the botanists. An example is E. Stillman Bailey's *The Sand Dunes of Indiana: The Story of an American Wonderland Told by Camera and Pen*, published in 1917. In it, Bailey proclaims,

> "To some, the dunes are uncomely— yellow, bothersome, changing sands, and nothing else. The gift of imagination was not bestowed on these people. They are to be pitied."[3]

But there were dunes-lovers in Indiana. Even the raw factory town of Gary was not without its pocket of culture and appreciation for nature; its Potawatomi Chapter of the D.A.R. in 1916 (when the town was only ten years old) passed a resolution calling for the creation of a park in the dunes. Lieber and the newly formed Indiana State Park Committee placed the dunes on their list of potential state parks, but movement for a national park quickly gathered momentum. Unfortunately, the entry of the United States into World War I turned the attention of Congress away from the acquisition of a few square miles in Indiana. After the war, supporters' hopes lay with the state. Their cries grew more urgent; resort development was now another threat along with that of encroaching factories.[4]

In every annual report of the Department of Conservation in the early 1920s, Lieber hammered on the desirability of the dunes as a state park. Finally in 1923 the General Assembly authorized a property tax toward the purchase of land for a park on the Lake Michigan shore in Porter County. The first tract acquired in 1925 contained the majestic Mount Tom dune, which had been coveted for its sand, not its beauty, by the industries to the west. (Sand is employed in the manufacture of coke, which is used in steel-making.) Donations from the likes of Elbert Gary's United States Steel Corporation sufficiently increased funds to purchase the remaining property most desired, including Waverly Beach.[5]

The South Shore continued to print brochures and advertising posters encouraging people to visit Indiana Dunes, and there was talk for a time of the railroad building a spur into the park. Within the boundaries was an old farmhouse, remodeled into the cozy Duneside Inn. In 1929 the park opened on Waverly Beach a stunning new two-story limestone pavilion, today one of the few surviving historic structures in the park. With Chicago traction magnate Samuel Insull's gift of a strip of land from the recently built Dunes Highway (present US12) to the South Shore tracks, Indiana Dunes was able to construct a new entrance road directly to the beach flanked by fortress-like limestone gatehouses that still stand. They are inscribed with inspirational snippets from poets Milton and Bryant, John Muir, and Francis Thompson, who composed Richard Lieber's favorite passage: "All things by immortal power near or far, hiddenly to each other linked are, that thou canst not stir a flower without troubling of a star." Shortly after, the three-story Arcade Hotel, designed by architect John Lloyd Wright, was erected immediately to the west of the Pavilion, as were additional cottages around Duneside Inn.[6]

The pavilion survives but the Arcade Hotel (left) was demolished in the early 1970s.

collection of Tom Hohman

In the fall of 1933 the New Deal came to the dunes in the form of CCC Company 556, who stayed until the following summer, when they moved on to Pokagon. The boys worked on roads, built a bridge across Dunes Creek, and constructed a large concrete reservoir to supply water to the campground. When Company 556 left, CCC Company 1563 from Medaryville came to the dunes and built a unique group camp with frame structures using what passed for Native

American motifs. The sleeping cabins were octagonal and resembled tipis. The CCC boys also built a new campground and improved the picnic grounds before Camp SP-5 was discontinued in the fall of 1935. The WPA briefly came into the park to build a pumphouse and, a few years later, a new sewage disposal system. To complete an ambitious new master plan drawn up in 1940, a new CCC camp was set up, but with the onset of World War II, it was never occupied, and the plans were shelved. During the war park employees salvaged material from the abandoned CCC barracks to construct two service buildings. Workers in the war industries of the Calumet region used the park heavily as a place to relieve their cares.[7]

The end of World War II did not signal a lessening of the tide of humanity that poured into the park. Then, as now, most of the visitors never got beyond the beach. Even in the 1950s the park sometimes had to close its gates because parking lots were full. Improvements to the property in the next two to three decades centered on replacing bridges and road surfaces subjected to heavy traffic and creating more room for automobiles and people within the park without sacrificing its unique environment. Overcrowded campgrounds were considerably enlarged. The group camp was very popular, and briefly in the 1960s a second group camp was housed at the Duneside Inn after it closed to the general public. All were torn down years ago, although the main group camp's dining hall was remodeled and used for a time as the park's nature center until the opening of the present building in 1990. The Arcade Hotel, later called the Dunes Hotel, closed after 1969 and was demolished a few years later. By that time the trend was to keep park inns open all year, and a hotel on the beach subjected to icy winds off the lake was not very popular in winter.[8]

In 2006 the Department of Natural Resources, supported by Governor Mitch Daniels and some tourism groups, put forward a plan to build a new hotel and conference center near the shoreline where the old hotel had been— although this building would be considerably larger. The proposal, which called for bids from private developers, met with considerable opposition from environmentalists and others who felt Indiana Dunes would suffer irretrievably from the even greater influx of people. The project was shelved. In a move unrelated to the hotel controversy, but in completely the opposite direction, the park took out the beach parking lot that was covering Dunes Creek, and is restoring the former wetland. In 2007, the park dedicated a new entrance, which restored the limestone gatehouses and the massive glacial rock that had historically rested between them. Over the years, despite the public demand for more space, the park has restricted development to the west end, leaving the eastern two-thirds as a nature preserve.[9]

The unique dunes environment includes wetlands with a variety of rare plants.

photo by GJ Greiff

Never truly dead, the movement for a national park was resurrected in the late 1950s with a heated standoff between proponents of preserving the shrunken remnant of the dunes outside the state park and those who wanted a major public port and the industrial growth that would accompany it. It seemed an either-or proposition until a compromise, which left no one truly happy, was effected in 1966, resulting in the Indiana Dunes National Lakeshore and the Burns Waterway Harbor.[10] The still-controversial National Lakeshore is discontiguous (but continues to expand piecemeal) and surrounds the state park.

The fact that the vast majority of visitors to Indiana Dunes hug the beach may be advantageous to nature lovers who wish to experience the many natural wonders of the dunes, although summertime can be steamy away from the lake. Autumn is best, with the rich colors of the oaks all around, and the brilliant blue of Lake Michigan free from the noisy throng. The lure of this rare landscape is difficult to describe; perhaps poet Carl Sandburg said it best: "The Dunes . . . constitute a signature of time and eternity."

Ever changing dunescape in Indiana Dunes State Park.

photo by GJ Greiff

 NOTES

1. "Conservation Report," 1920, 299.

2. W.S. Blatchley, "The Geology of Lake and Porter Counties," in *Twenty-Second Annual Report of Indiana Department of Geology and Natural Resources* (Indianapolis: Wm. E. Burford Company, 1898), 33-41; See E. Stillman Bailey, *The Sand Dunes of Indiana: The Story of an American Wonderland Told by Camera and Pen* (Chicago: A.C. McClurg & Company, 1917), passim; George S. Cottman, *The Indiana Dunes State Park* (Indianapolis: Department of Conservation, 1930), 30.

3. Bailey, *The Sand Dunes of Indiana*, 24-25, see also 159-160; Cottman, *Indiana Dunes*, 35; George A. Brennan, *The Wonders of the Dunes* (Indianapolis: Bobbs-Merrill Company, 1923), 163-164.

4. See Cottman, *Indiana Dunes State Park*, 35-37; Brennan, *Wonders of the Dunes*, 163-175.

5. See "Conservation Reports," 1920-1925, passim; Cottman, *Indiana Dunes State Park*, 36-39; "Waverly Beach Is Bought by State," *Indianapolis News*, 22 December 1925; "Large Gifts Further Dunes Park Project," *Indianapolis News*, 11 January 1926.

6. "Conservation Reports," 1927, 654; 1931, 866; see Cottman, *Indiana Dunes State Park*, 39-41. See also *Indiana Dunes State Park* (Brochure produced by the Department of Conservation ca. 1933). The Thompson passage is also inscribed on Lieber's grave monument at Turkey Run.

7. Information gleaned from RG35, E115 "Camp Inspection Reports," Box 71, Indiana SP5, Chesterton, NA; "Conservation Reports, 1934-1944, passim; "Medaryville C.C.C. Boys Erect Unique Scout Camp," *Pulaski County Democrat*, 4 July 1935.

8. See Ray Gregg, "Dunes State Park Offers State an 'Ocean' Beach," *South Bend Tribune*, State Park Edition, 1948. Information on development from "Conservation Reports," 1960, I-56; 1963, 8; "DNR Reports," 1972, 75; 1979, 139.

9. Jeff Fleischer, "Development on the Dunes, " *Chicago Wilderness Magazine*, Fall 2006, http://chicagowildernessmag.org/issues/fall2006/dunes.html; Interview, Bortner, 20 May 2008; "New Entrance to Indiana Dunes to Be Dedicated," *InsideINdianaBusiness.Com*, 27 June 2007, http//www.insideindianabusiness.com/newsitem.asp?ID==24119#middle.

10. See "Indiana's Vast Dunes that Survived Eons of Time Face Possible Extinction," *Eastern Sun*, 26 December 1957; Gordon Englehart, "The Disputed Dunes," *Louisville Courier-Journal Magazine*, 23 July 1961, 7-11; Englehart, "Indiana Dunes: Controversial Sands of Time," *Louisville Courier-Journal Magazine*, 3 April 1966, 29-41. See also Ralph D. Gray, *Public Ports for Indiana: A History of the Indiana Port Commission* (Indianapolis: Indiana Historical Bureau, 1988), especially chapters 2-5.

POKAGON STATE PARK
(Established 1925)

Although it might come as a surprise to most visitors, Pokagon State Park was largely unforested when the Department of Conservation took possession of the six hundred original acres of farmland and orchard—the Failing estate—in 1925. The motivation behind its acquisition—besides the fact that Steuben County offered it as a gift to the state—was to assure public access in perpetuity to one of northern Indiana's loveliest glacially formed waters, Lake James.

The Department of Conservation opened what was briefly called Lake James State Park the following year, beginning development with a picnic area and some trails. The park's new name honored Leopold Pokagon and his son Simon, chiefs of the Potawatomi tribe of native Americans that once inhabited the area. Construction began on a large inn above the southernmost basin of the lake, which opened in 1927 as the Potawatomi Inn. The establishment of two beaches proved a strong draw, and improved campgrounds were soon developed at the north end of the

A view of Pokagon in the early 1930s, before the CCC planted thousands of trees.

Pokagon State Park archives

park. Despite Richard Lieber's continual celebration of the virtues of interacting with nature, the Inn offered such cultural delights as Sunday afternoon band concerts, which were very popular. By the 1930s a craft shop at the Inn offered instruction to visitors inclined to less vigorous pursuits than hiking and swimming. Large animal pens containing several elk and bison were another attempt to enlighten the public, a precursor to the nature center built nearby over fifty years later in 1981. (The pens are now gone, removed in the early 1990s.) The beginnings of a boys camp appeared in the early 1930s on a bluff overlooking the upper basin of the lake, built in part through a Civil Works Administration project.[1]

The original lobby of the Potawatomi Inn has not greatly changed in decades.

collection of Tom Hohman

CCC Company 556 finished its work at the Indiana Dunes and established Camp SP-7 at Pokagon in 1934. The park underwent an ambitious development program, which included reforestation, landscaping, road building, and construction of numerous outdoor recreational facilities. CCC boys hewed local timber and split native stone to construct buildings that harmonized especially well with the park environment, in keeping with guidelines created by the National Park Service. Perhaps the best example is the beautiful two-story shelterhouse (now called

71

the "CCC Shelter") that nestles in the woods above the beach. Most of the park's landscaping and present buildings—including the old gatehouse, the saddle barn, the dining hall and much of the group camp, and the bath house—are the work of the CCC, which remained in the park until January 1942. They also built the first toboggan slide, which has since been rebuilt and remodeled several times. Pokagon is the site of the first and longest-running annual CCC reunion in the country, beginning with the first in 1953. The park owes much to those youthful workers who shaped the land so many years ago. Over the years, the stories these men told have provided valuable information and enriched the park's archives.[2]

In the decades following World War II, the rampant growth of family camping activity caused Pokagon to construct more and expand the existing campgrounds to the point of saturation. In the early 1990s the park reconfigured its campgrounds, resulting in fewer but more attractive sites. Public response was favorable and prompted the Division to do the same in other parks. The Potawatomi Inn has been expanded numerous times. With all its many additions and remodelings, the most recent in 1995, the original portion still maintains its character and its

Originally constructed by the CCC and substantially rehabilitated, this bridge carries a county road unobtrusively through the park.

photo by GJ Greiff

views of the lake. Other than the ever-increasing overnight accommodations and the new nature center, relatively little has been added or changed at the park. Consequently, most of Pokagon State Park is listed in the National Register of Historic Places.

Pokagon is immensely popular with vacationers year around, what with the cooling waters of Lake James in summer and the toboggan slide that draws huge crowds on winter weekends. But for reflective walks the park's matured forests offer carpets of delicate woodland flowers in spring and glorious autumnal colors amidst the lovely rolling terrain of northern Indiana.[3]

NOTES

1. Information on development gleaned from R1933 030530 "National Park Service—State Park Division," Folder "CCC-CWA-PWA etc. Lands and Water," SA: "Conservation Reports," 1925-1934, passim; "DNR Report," 1981, 175.

2. See Greiff, "New Deal Resources"; also, Greiff, "Nomination Form for Pokagon State Park Historic District," National Register of Historic Places, 1995.

The combination shelter ("CCC Shelter") is listed in the National Register of Historic Places. In 1996, most of the park was listed in the National Register as a historic district representing the work of the CCC.

3. Interview, Pagac, 3 February 1993; conversation with Randy White, park manager, 11 April 1995.

SPRING MILL STATE PARK
(Established 1927)

In 1817 brothers Thomas and Cuthbert Bullitt purchased a large tract of land in what would become Lawrence County and immediately began constructing a large stone grist mill. Some eight years later Hugh and Thomas Hamer acquired the mill, about which some dwellings of artisans and workers had already clustered. Typical of pioneer entrepreneurs, the Hamers over the years expanded into other small businesses, mostly centered on the mill. The hamlet at first was called Arcola and acquired a post office in 1828; three years later it became Spring Mill. For a few decades the little town flourished, but its good fortune gradually waned after the railroads passed it by in the 1850s; the government closed the post office in 1859. An epidemic of smallpox killed its chief mover and shaker, Hugh Hamer, in the 1870s, and the mill passed out of the family a few years later. By the mid-1890s the hamlet was deserted. Much has been made of the village's abandonment, but this was certainly not unusual in the nineteenth century (nor even today), and virtually every Indiana county may speak of a lost town or two. The lack of commerce and a main transportation line was quite sufficient to kill such a tiny settlement, and nearby Mitchell, with its railroad, was growing.[1]

In 1865 George Donaldson, a wealthy and eccentric Scot who spent much of his life traveling the world's wilds, purchased close to two hundred acres of heavily wooded and cave-pocked land in the vicinity of the Hamer village. When not traveling or at one of his several estates elsewhere, he dwelt in a curio-filled cottage surrounded by the patch of old growth forest (now Donaldson's Woods Nature Preserve) that Donaldson resolutely forbade to be disturbed. Around 1882, while Donaldson was away on one of his long trips, vandals damaged or destroyed outbuildings and fences, burned the quaintly named Shawnee Cottage, and stole its contents. The peripatetic Scot never returned and put the property up for sale. But no one bought the land, and when Donaldson died intestate in 1898, the state —in the form of Indiana University—ultimately received the property, which was used for a biological laboratory. In 1927 the General Assembly authorized funds to pay the university for the upkeep of the former Donaldson land on condition that other parties, such as Lawrence County, would donate additional contiguous acreage to the state for a park.[2]

After the turn of the century the ruins of the mill and the remnants of the deserted village of Spring Mill had become a popular picnic spot for

The restored and recreated village includes the Hamer Mill and several log structures, many of which were moved in and rebuilt on site in the 1920s and 1930s.

photo by GJ Greiff

73

Mitchell area residents. The Lehigh Portland Cement Company had secured most of the valley in which the ruins rested in order to protect their water source, the very stream that once powered the mill. The company donated nearly three hundred acres that included the village to the Department of Conservation, on condition it be used for a park and that Lehigh retain its water rights. Richard Lieber had already been very pleased at the prospect of a state park comprised of Donaldson's primeval forest and cave topography. But "far more thrilling" was the "discovery of the historical significance of Spring Mill village" on the new tract, remnants of a typical pioneer settlement such as he had long hoped to recreate.[3]

The 1820s Granny White House was moved to the Spring Mill site under Richard Lieber's direction.

collection of GJ Greiff

Almost immediately Lieber began restoration of what remained of the old village, clearing out the accumulated scrub and removing a more modern residence, and most importantly, rehabilitating the mill. The Granny White house was moved in from the Leesville area several miles to the northeast. More were brought in or reconstructed from ruins. The village is a mix of original buildings that were on the site supplemented with relocated, mostly nineteenth century structures that are interpreted as buildings appropriate to the place and time. As for the park proper, workers constructed the basics: two picnic areas, a small campground, a custodian's cottage and a service building.[4]

Other than the main work of re-creating the village, little development took place at Spring Mill until the New Deal. The first to be quartered in an Indiana state park, CCC Company 1536 occupied Camp SP-1 in June 1933. While CCC companies normally were segregated, this one was unusual in that it was integrated with about eight percent black enrollees. It is probable that the work details would have been segregated, and that all the young black men were housed in one barracks building, but the records do not make a point of this. The CCC boys immediately set to work building roads and an earth dam and spillway for a thirty-acre lake. They were joined in November 1934 by a black company just come from Yellowstone, Company 539, which set up Camp SP-10. The new company worked at Spring Mill a little over a year before going on to a new camp outside Evansville. Despite the project superintendent's occasional references to the "different habits and natures of the two races," and his assertion that the "negro race requires a different method of supervision and handling," several major projects were completed during the period both companies were at work in the park.[5] Company 539 was, after all, comprised of experienced workers fresh from Yellowstone, not new recruits. There had been no such racial prejudices evident in earlier narrative reports of the integrated—or "mixed," as it was called in the reports—Company 1536; indeed, its "high morale" was often noted. A beautifully designed triple-arch bridge over the west end of the unfinished lake was the most impressive accomplishment; the CCC built none other like it in Indiana. They erected two large shelter houses, numerous ovens and a comfort station for the new picnic grounds above Donaldson Cave, and a wonderfully unobtrusive restroom building resembling a log cabin in a quiet corner of the village area.[6]

After the second company left, the boys of Company 1536 went on to complete the restoration they had begun on the Bullitt House, which was the only structure in the village that the CCC worked on, although they did a great deal of the landscaping. They built a new campground with all the improvements near the picnic area, three multi-unit overnight cabins, and an attractive stone-and-timber boathouse at the extreme west edge of the still unfinished lake. Not far from the village, the former boathouse is today a shelter house, with the lake now several hundred yards away. The boys razed the old Camp SP-10 and used the lumber to build picnic tables. The Department began construction on a new limestone hotel in 1937. The CCC did not work on the building itself, but did excavating and landscaping, as well as constructing the road to the hotel and a large parking lot. The Spring Mill Inn opened in 1939 and hosted the annual National Conference on State Parks the following year. Among the CCC's last projects was the new entrance development on the south edge of the park with a gatehouse and a road leading from the new SR60 that was then itself under construction.[7]

Until the gatehouse as moved deeper into the park, lines of cars often extended onto the highway.

photo by GJ Greiff

WPA workers took on some additional projects at Spring Mill, starting in 1938. They installed a new water system, reconditioned furnishings for the village, and began to erect a bath house on the new lake. The CCC worked on the bath house as well, but their camp was discontinued in early 1941. With the onset of World War II, the bath house was one of the New Deal projects that had be abandoned, but park employees completed the job the following year. Today the remodeled structure houses Spring Mill's nature center.[8] The manmade lake has continued to fill in over time, and the prospect was that the dam would be removed in the future and the stream and its flood plain ultimately returned to something approximating the original state. At present, the possibility of reestablishing the lake is under consideration with the help of outside funds.

While certainly some visitors came to admire the mighty trees or tour one of the interesting caves on the property, the village is no doubt what made Spring Mill State Park so widely known around the country. Intrigued by the Brigadoon-like town come back to life, a growing number of people flocked to the village to eat at the tavern, admire the crafts, and often, carry home their little sack of ground corn from the mill. The grain, craft items, and food offered for sale in the village created a healthy income source for Spring Mill. Interpretation of the village has continued to change with further research into early nineteenth century life, at times aided by a staff historian. The park also started to create special events—candlelight tours, autumn and Christmas festivals—to bring even more people to the village, and these have been very successful.

In 1960 the park added a permanent saddle barn of functional design northeast of Donaldson's Woods, where a temporary stable had stood. To the north of it were developed a range of camping facilities, modern and primitive, and also a youth tent area. The former campground in the main part of the park is now a picnic ground. The development boom of the 1970s also brought a new swimming pool and bath house, not far from the burgeoning campground. The Inn underwent remodeling and added a pool as well. Spring Mill's growth and popularity ultimately resulted in traffic hazards at the entrance, with long lines of cars backed up onto the highway. The solution, realized in the early 1990s, was to move the gatehouse well back into the park. More recently, in response to public demand, the park has created trails for mountain bike users.[9]

The Grissom Memorial honors one of the original Mercury 7 astronauts who was a native of nearby Mitchell. _photo by GJ Greiff_

In 1967 the General Assembly authorized the establishment of the Virgil I. Grissom Memorial Visitors Center at Spring Mill to honor one of the nation's first astronauts. Although not directly linked to the park, Grissom, tragically killed while training for a lunar flight, was a native of nearby Mitchell and had often visited Spring Mill. Construction of the memorial began a few years later, and Governor Whitcomb dedicated the Grissom Memorial in the summer of 1972. It houses a small museum that includes Grissom's famous "Molly Brown" Gemini space capsule.[10]

While the village in season is a worthwhile visit, a quiet walk amidst the shuttered buildings on a late fall or early spring day has its own charms. Indeed, Spring Mill offers a myriad of beautiful hikes for the hardy; the most awe-inspiring, perhaps, is through the rare stand of massive trees in Donaldson's Woods.

 NOTES

1. Indiana Post Office Index, cards 252-253, on file at Indiana Division, ISL; see Norman C. Evans, _Spring Mill (Hidden Valley Village): The Story of Southern Indiana's Pioneer Village_ (Mill Lake Press, 1953), 13-54; "Water Wheel and Mill Machinery at Spring Mill Authentic Reproductions," _Outdoor Indiana_ 2 (February 1935), 18. "Spring Mill—Oasis of Peace," _Outdoor Indiana_ 4 (November 1937), 12-13. Sources, of which there are many, vary on fine details and dates of the town's abandonment.

2. See "Conservation Report," 1927, 655; Evans, *Hidden Valley Village*, 115-126; "Proposed New State Park Will Open One of Nature's Choicest Gold Spots," *Indianapolis Star*, 10 April 1927; Bessie Lynn Hufford, "George Donaldson, Whose Farm Now Is an Indiana Park, Was a Mysterious Man, Little Known Until After his Death in Scotland," *Indianapolis Star*, 16 June 1929. See also Steven Higgs, "George Donaldson: Spring Mill's Eccentric Naturalist," *Traces* 5 (Summer 1993), 28-37.

3. Lieber quoted in "Conservation Report," 1928, 246; see "288 Acres Given for State Park," *Indianapolis Star*, 6 July 1928; Evans, *Hidden Valley Village*, 133, 143; Mohammed Ansari, *A History of Spring Mill Village* (unpublished manuscript funded by Indiana Committee for the Humanities, 1985), 143. Lieber had been planning to create a pioneer village at Turkey Run State Park, but abandoned that site in favor of the newly acquired Spring Mill property.

4. Information on development gleaned from "Conservation Reports," 1929-1932, passim.

5. Quotations from Ernest E. Walker, Senior Project Superintendent, "Spring Mill SP-10: Monthly Narrative and Pictorial Report for November, 1934," (Mitchell, Indiana, 30 November 1934).

The report also notes that more of the black enrollees had graduated from high school than had the white enrollees, but dismissed this fact by asserting that "academic training is not necessarily an index to the amount of honest work which will be accomplished," indeed, [in a fantastic twist of reasoning] "it may be used as a method to evade work."

6. Information gleaned from RG35, E115 "Camp Inspection Reports," Box 71 (SP-1), Box 72, (SP-10), NA; "Conservation Reports," 1934-1936, passim.

7. Work of the CCC gleaned from RG35, E115 "Camp Inspection Reports," Box 71 (SP-1), NA; "Conservation Reports," 1935-1942, passim.

8. See "Conservation Reports," 1938-1942, passim; "Six WPA Jobs Are Approved," *Indianapolis Times*, 19 October 1939.

9. Information on development gleaned from "Conservation Reports," 1960-1964, passim, and "DNR Reports," 1965-1980, passim.

10. See "Conservation Reports," 1960, I-65; 1964, 36; "DNR Reports," 1967, 25; 1970, 4; 1972, 78.

BROWN COUNTY STATE PARK
(Established 1929)

Our largest state park—indeed, one of the ten largest state parks in the nation—lies in the heart of and is named for Brown County. Comprised of about twenty-five square miles of wooded hills from which one may overlook the surrounding forested knobs, the park's mystique surpasses its much-vaunted beauty. Its forests that blaze in the fall, drawing thousands of tourists to line the park roads bumper to bumper while gaping at the "color," are relatively young. Most were planted by the CCC on submarginal farmland that had been cultivated as late as the 1920s with mule-drawn single-bladed plows. Nearly all the original forest but for a few inaccessible areas had succumbed to commercial and private lumbering in the nineteenth century. But Richard Lieber himself was drawn to the area's lovely pockets of scenery, and declared as early as 1910 during a visit to a friend's rustic getaway in Brown County that it ought to be preserved as a state park for everyone to enjoy. Others agreed. Passing through Indiana in 1915, prominent conservationist Enos Mills declared that the state should purchase as much land as possible deep in Brown County, for it was "purely wild . . . one of the best spots . . . between the Appalachians and the Rocky Mountains."[1]

The fire tower on Weed Patch Hill offers spectacular views of the park.

collection of Tom Hohman

In 1924 the Department of Conservation began to buy up tracts for Indiana's first game preserve southeast of Nashville, an isolated county seat hamlet that had for some years harbored an artists' colony. The Division of Fish and Game planted food crops to draw and nurture game birds, started reforestation, built a fire tower, and constructed a dam to form a ten-acre lake. In 1929 the Brown County Commissioners donated an adjoining tract of land on the north for a state park, an action authorized by the General Assembly two years before. Originally, the county had offered two parcels, one north and one south of the game preserve. The two divisions involved and the county commissioners came to a trade agreement, and the southernmost parcel went to Fish and Game. Part of that division's property on the north then went to Lands and Waters for the park. It included Weed Patch Hill, long a popular picnic spot, where the Department had erected a fire tower. After two years of minimal development and the construction of an entrance and roadway, Brown County State Park opened in 1931.[2]

78

Lieber chose Brown County for his "family housekeeping experiment," the idea being to keep accommodations simple and prices modest, something between the primitive pleasures of camping and the comparative luxury of a state park inn. The Abe Martin Lodge was set atop Kin Hubbard Ridge, named for the Hoosier humorist who created the popular *Abe Martin* cartoon. Twenty rustic housekeeping cabins, each named for one of Hubbard's rube characters, were clustered nearby and opened in 1932 to immediate success. The following year both a saddle barn and a new swimming pool began operation, the latter indicative of the Division's commitment to developing water features in state parks, which the public highly favored. Expensive to build and maintain, pools were rare in state parks before World War II; McCormick's Creek was the only other that could boast of one.[3]

This covered bridge, built in Putnam County in 1838, was moved to the north park entrance in 1932.
photo by GJ Greiff

As the State Highway Commission was struggling to create a network of improved roads for Indiana's burgeoning automobile population, an unusual two-lane covered bridge, built in 1838 on an early state road near Fincastle in Putnam County, was threatened with demolition. The state moved the bridge some fifty miles to the north entrance road of Brown County State Park in 1932; it is the oldest existing wooden covered bridge in Indiana, albeit not in its original setting.[4]

Brown County State Park opened in the midst of the Depression, and its early development benefited greatly from the New Deal. In the winter of 1933-1934 a Civil Works Administration project worked out of Strahl Valley in the southeast part of the property. Some of the men and their families took temporary housing in the few remaining dwellings of the abandoned village of Kelp, already waning at the time the Department of Conservation purchased the land. During their brief stay, CWA workers toiled clearing trails and constructing shelters.[5]

In 1933 unemployed World War I veterans formed two CCC companies, 1557 and 1561, and the next year established a camp at Brown County State Park, actually located within the game preserve. The men of the CCC carried on a variety of projects that laid a foundation for the park as we know it today. Among the earliest projects undertaken were the nearly identical north and west gatehouses, resembling rustic cabins typical of the surrounding county. Throughout the formidable terrain, the CCC built the park's basic infrastructure: water supply, sewage disposal, service roads and trails, along with shelters and fireplace ovens. From the time Brown County State Park opened to the public, visitors wandered freely into the game preserve area as well. To accommodate them, the CCC constructed an exhibit shelter, called the "vermin house," to help educate people about animals from the surrounding forests and fields—and also to help keep the public away from the brooding and nesting areas. Thirty years later, the park remodeled the structure into the recreation building that now serves Buffalo Ridge campground. Another favorite destination for curious park visitors was the CCC camp itself farther south on Lookout Point. A picnic ground today marks the area.[6]

Using native sandstone quarried on the property, the CCC constructed an open-air amphitheater not far from the Lodge as a place for programs and entertainment. Down the hill the workers built the largest saddle barn of any Indiana state park, with stalls for 25 horses, replacing the one built only a few years earlier by park employees. (The original saddle barn still stands, about 150 yards south of the present one that the CCC constructed.) Other CCC projects in the park included the attractive two-story Lower Shelter nudged against a hillside, the Upper Shelter, the West Lookout, and Ogle Lake. With dwindling enrollment due to stepped-up war industries, one of the CCC camps was discontinued in 1941, but work continued in the park until the end of the program in early 1942.[7]

The largest saddle barn in any of the state parks, built by the CCC in 1936.

collection of GJ Greiff

In 1941 the Department decided the best use of the two adjacent properties, as far as serving the public was concerned, was to consolidate the park and the game preserve to create one large state park. Functionally, the game farm had been virtually abandoned as the state established propagation facilities on new properties elsewhere. Hence, with some financial reimbursement going to the Division of Fish and Game, the holdings of Brown County State Park suddenly quadrupled. The park retained and even expanded the animal exhibits in the 1950s to include large display pens, since visitors seemed to enjoy them, but eventually the area was needed for other purposes. With Brown County's rugged terrain, space for development is limited. The park found a place to construct an interpretive nature center—the first in the system—in 1969, and later an amphitheater behind it for the well attended programs presented by the naturalist. In more recent years, with the growth in popularity of mountain bikes, the park has opened several miles of trails geared towards them.[8]

Like all of the state parks, Brown County was caught in the campground crunch, brought on by the tremendous growth of interest in family camping in the 1950s and the public's desire for more modern campsites. The park had little in the way of improved camping facilities until the development in the 1960s of the family and horsemen's campgrounds, which have been expanded considerably over the years. More cabins were built in the Abe Martin complex in the 1950s, but it was not until the late 1960s that the park added hotel rooms to the Lodge itself. The most recent family housekeeping units in the park, built in the 1980s, are of modern design with balconies and expansive windows. In response to contemporary tastes in public recreation, the Abe Martin Lodge opened for its guests an indoor water park in 2008.[9]

Brown County remains phenomenally popular with vacationers, many of whom leave the park to prowl the shops of Nashville and environs. The county depends on tourism to survive. Those who come to Brown County to give up their cares to the forest will find the park large enough to allow them space, except perhaps in autumn when the annual hordes of "leafers" (as the natives call them) descend.

Nestled into a hillside, this stone-and-timber shelterhouse was built by World War I veterans enrolled in the CCC.

photo by GJ Greiff

 NOTES

1. "Creation of State Parks Advocated," *Indianapolis News*, 17 November 1915; E. Lieber, *Richard Lieber*, 68-69; see James P. Eagelman, "Washington Township: The Brown County Forest Story from 1780 to 1980," (Master's thesis, Depauw University, 1980), 78-79.

Lieber was sufficiently entranced with Brown County to buy land and build a retreat near that of his friend Fred Hetherington in Jackson Township.

2. Information on acquisition from "Conservation Reports," 1924, 186; 1925, 326; 1926, 290; 1928, 162-163, 249; 1929, 142, 251-252; 1930, 434, 543-544; 1931, 879. "Brown County State Park," *Indianapolis Star*, 22 September 1923. See also Eagelman, 90-94.

3. Information on development from "Conservation Reports," 1932, 369, 378; 1933, 383-384, 391.

4. "Conservation Report," 1933, 391.

5. RG 79, Box 206, document establishing CWA project in Brown County, NA; see William Herschell, "Indiana, Now October-Minded, Centers Interest in Old Brown County," *Indianapolis News*, 20 October 1934.

6. RG35, E115, "Camp Inspection Reports," Boxes 68 and 72, NA; *Indiana District, Civilian Conservation Corps, 1938-1939*, 72-73; "Improve State Game Preserve," *Outdoor Indiana* 1 (July 1934), 20. See Greiff, *Walking Through Time: A History Hike in Brown County State Park*, narrative for audio walking tour produced in 1991, on file at Indiana Humanties Council Resource Center and available at the Abe Martin Lodge. See also "Conservation Reports," 1963, 9.

7. Greiff, *Walking Through Time*; "Conservation Reports," 1941, 961; 1942, 171.

8. See "Conservation Reports," 1941, 916, 961; 1956, 4; "DNR Report," 1969, 1.

9. See "DNR Reports," 1965, 2; 1968, 5; 1969, 1; 1975, 101.

SHAKAMAK STATE PARK
(Acquired 1929)

Despite the high standards of scenic beauty Richard Lieber had established for state parks, he recognized the great need for a place of recreational escape in the hardscrabble coal mining region of southwestern Indiana. Therefore, as an experiment he accepted in 1929 a gift of over a thousand acres from Greene, Clay, and Sullivan counties. This land, where the three counties abutted, was far from pristine. But it offered immediate possibilities for an artificial lake, which could be dammed by adapting an abandoned railroad grade across a creek valley. Workers filled in a culvert and constructed a spillway impounding a lake of about 55 acres that covered some abandoned shaft mines. Beach development followed, including a small bath house. On higher ground on the other side, a group camp was begun, administered by regional 4-H clubs. The park opened to visitors in 1930 and was named for the nearby Shakamak River. The word comes from the Kickapoo, who once dwelt in the region, and means "river of the long fish," or eel. People flocked to the park, which erected six housekeeping cabins overlooking the lake in 1932, following the success of those opened in Brown County that year.[1]

Shakamak still had a long way to go before it could take its place with the other parks in the system. Fortunately several New Deal programs were soon available to hasten the process. A Civil Works Administration project employed several hundred local men in the winter of 1933-34 to work on trails and shelters, all "centered around the proposed new lake" southeast of the first. The duration of the CWA was too brief for the workers to complete the necessary dam, but the Federal Emergency Relief Administration funded further work on it. Workers also constructed fish rearing ponds as a means to keep the lakes stocked and built a pen for large birds and corrals to display deer, elk, and bison. By 1937 the Works Progress Administration completed the animal exhibits, fish hatchery, and the reservoir project, first called Lake Jason and later named Lake Lenape.[2]

CCC Company 522 occupied the buildings of the group camp in November 1933, establishing Camp SP-3. Four years later they built a regular CCC camp northwest of the group camp, freeing it for public use again. The CCC boys constructed the main park roads, worked on foot trails and built six new group camp buildings and more family cabins. They planted hundreds of thousands of trees that have since matured into a lovely forest. CCC workers developed a picnic area with shelters west of the first lake and built a fine

View of the former bath house (today the Nature Center) across Lake Shakamak.

photo by GJ Greiff

brick-and-timber shelterhouse near the beach. As clay was plentiful and much used in this region, the choice of brick—indeed, a native material—for many of the park structures reflected the history of the area. Another project that highlighted the park's natural history was the creation of an educational exhibit where an abandoned coal drift was visible near a trail. The park discontinued the coal mine exhibit decades ago; the remnant of it, visible off Trail 2, is often mistaken for a former mine. Other results of the CCC's eight-year presence in the park include the gatehouse and the saddle barn. South of the beach they built a campground that was used for many years but has since been vacated, and part of the site was inundated by a third lake in the 1960s. A new bath house that involved both CCC and WPA workers was left unfinished when America's entry into World War II ended the New Deal. Park employees completed the bath house and also remodeled some of the CCC camp buildings into family cabins. A brick hotel had been part of Shakamak's master plan in the late 1930s, but it never came to fruition. The termination of federal work projects was a factor, but housekeeping cabins and campsites may have seemed more appropriate to this park; certainly that had been Lieber's feeling when the Department acquired Shakamak. The park constructed several more cabins during the 1950s.[3]

With the acquisition in the 1960s of over seven hundred acres of land to the southwest, Shakamak, in cooperation with the USDA's Soil Conservation Service,

The brick-and-timber saddle barn constructed by CCC Company 522 in the 1930s.

photo by GJ Greiff

impounded yet another body of water. Lake Kickapoo, as it was named, was three times the size of the earlier two combined and located between them, making one large expanse of water. The old dam creating Lake Lenape became a roadway that crossed over and led park visitors around the new lake. The road also provided access to the new campground on the south side of Lake Lenape. Much of the original campground (along with the old animal pens and fish rearing ponds) was flooded by the new lake. What remained of the old campground became a picnic area in the early 1980s. The multiple waters of Shakamak State Park continue to draw thousands of anglers each year.[4]

Beginning in 1935, when the CCC had constructed a ten-meter diving tower, Shakamak for decades hosted swimming and diving championship meets each summer, sanctioned by the Amateur Athletic Association. Ironically, the lovely Lake Shakamak, once nationally known for its swimming facilities, is no longer open for that activity because of the presence of dangerous bacteria in the water. Today, park visitors frolic instead in the huge family pool in sight of the old beach.[5]

Most of the north and east sections of Shakamak State Park form a district that is listed in the National Register of Historic Places because of the wealth of New Deal projects still extant. Despite its origins as land in a highly disturbed state, Shakamak today, very much a planned landscape, is heavily wooded, an attractive mature forest surrounding picturesque expanses of open water. In spring, a lovely time to wander the park, hikers find a flower-carpeted woodland and, if alert, may hear Pan piping in the distance.

 NOTES

1. See "Conservation Reports," 1929, 251; 1930, 543; 1931, 880; 1932, 379; Tom Wallace, *Over the River: Indiana State Parks and Memorials* (Indianapolis: Department of Conservation, 1932), 43; Russell F. Abdill, *Shakamak State Park* (Indianapolis: Department of Conservation, 1931), 3-11; "Engineering Problems at Shakamak Included Safeguarding Water Supply," *Outdoor Indiana* 1 (November 1934), 17, 26.

2. See "Conservation Reports," 1934, 551-552; 1935, 462-463; 1936, 414-415; 1937, 810-811; Greiff, comp., "Potential WPA Historic Properties in Indiana," (HLFI 1988), 10; "Engineering Problems at Shakamak," 17, 26.

3. Information on the work of the CCC found in RG35, "Camp Inspection Reports," Box 71; RG79, E-37, "State Park Files," Box 206, NA; "Conservation Reports," 1934, 551-552; 1935, 462-463; 1936, 414-415; 1937, 810-811; 1938, 902-903; 1939, 818-819; 1940, 356. See also "Engineering Problems at Shakamak," 17, 26; "Shakamak State Park Possesses Varied Attractions Centering Around Lakes," *Outdoor Indiana* 6 (August 1939), 15-18.

4. See "DNR Reports," 1969, 1; 1982, 199; K.W. Harris, "Shakamak State Park Expands," *Outdoor Indiana* 32 (December 1966-January 1967), 24-25.

5. See "A.A.U. Championship Swimming Meet to Be Held at Shakamak State Park," *Outdoor Indiana* 3 (August 1936), 3; "Shakamak State Park Possesses Varied Attractions," 17; "Swimming and Diving Championships at Shakamak State Park," *Outdoor Indiana* 9 (July 1942), 1, 12.

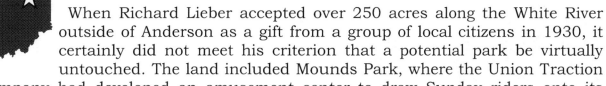

MOUNDS STATE PARK
(Acquired 1930)

When Richard Lieber accepted over 250 acres along the White River outside of Anderson as a gift from a group of local citizens in 1930, it certainly did not meet his criterion that a potential park be virtually untouched. The land included Mounds Park, where the Union Traction Company had developed an amusement center to draw Sunday riders onto its interurban cars. But the park's boundaries enclosed a number of prehistoric mounds worthy of preservation that were in danger of being lost to development. The Depression was the final blow causing the failure of the interurban company, and many feared that the earthworks, constructed by the Adena and Hopewell cultures some two thousand years before, might be obliterated, as indeed, some had been already. Builders had unwittingly dug a road—now old SR67—right through one; the carousel in Mounds Park had stood in the middle of a rare "fiddle-back" mound and hordes of amusement seekers had worn down some smaller earthworks. Still, for the most part the bluffs above the river, where the mounds appear to be concentrated, remained intact.[1]

That the majority of the mounds had survived until the interurban company purchased the land in the 1890s owes much to an early settler of Madison County, Frederick Bronnenberg, Jr., whose two-story brick dwelling dating to the 1840s still stands on the property. The structure housed the park's nature center for several years, but today the historic building, listed in the National Register of Historic Places, is interpreted as a mid-nineteenth century farmhouse when tours are offered. More restoration is planned, and archaeologists have uncovered evidence of several outbuildings. Within the park's boundaries are eleven identified earthworks, the most notable being the Great Mound, which underwent scientific excavations in the late 1960s. Archaeologists discovered burial remains, tools of bone and stone, projectile points, and fragments of pottery. Subsequent excavations continue to reveal more information about the earthworks, including the fact they appear to relate to astronomical phenomena.[2]

The first order of business after the Division acquired the land in 1930 was to clear away the remnants of the pleasure resort, especially around the earthworks. Mounds State Park opened the next year, and workers were busy building hiking trails, a road through the park, and a pavilion, which would provide meal service and a gathering place, on the edge of a bluff. They remodeled an existing dwelling for the custodian's residence and began developing picnic and

The pavilion was built shortly after the state acquired the park in 1930.

photo by GJ Greiff

85

A walk through the woods at Mounds takes on a mystical quality in the late fall light.

photo by GJ Greiff

camping areas. Although Mounds State Park was relatively small, plans to develop it were ambitious. In a forest clearing, the park built a log house in 1933 and surrounded it with appropriate plantings, beginning what was intended eventually to represent a complete pioneer homestead with all the outbuildings. The Federal Emergency Relief Administration (FERA) program of the New Deal provided some of the workers for this project as well as for the construction of a new saddle barn in 1935. So popular was horseback riding on the park's wooded trails that only two years later the WPA doubled the saddle barn and constructed a new riding ring. They also built an attractive entrance and brick gatehouse. None of these structures remain. In 1941, the National Youth Administration (NYA), a sort of junior WPA, set up a residential camp and a workshop in the park at the north end of the property, which was vacated the following year. NYA workers developed trails and helped with some of the construction projects in the park.[3]

World War II brought an end to further major projects at Mounds. But for the most part, all the space that could reasonably be developed in the park was taken up, and as the decades passed, needs and priorities changed. A large swimming pool and bath house complex, dedicated in 1982, is sited in the area where the pioneer homestead and saddle barn once stood. A small campground remains, but aside from the lure of the swimming pool, picnicking and hiking are the chief delights at Mounds. Near the pool, volunteers have created a butterfly garden and the park has been designated an official monarch butterfly way station. Proximity to Anderson can intrude upon one's sense of closeness to nature, and at times a solitary walk through the forest is likely to be much interrupted by local joggers and cross-country trainers; Mounds functions largely as a city park.

Still, in early spring the wooded bluffs of Mounds State Park are a fine place to hear the earth awaken. Countless springs and rills dot the ravines, and rivulets dance down the hillsides, sidling around and over recalcitrant icicles into the swollen rush of White River. As the wind whispers through the leafless oaks, one can catch something of the spirit that lingers amidst the mounds.

 NOTES

1. See "Conservation Report," 1930, 538; *The Mound Builders of Indiana and Mounds State Park* (Indianapolis: Department of Conservation, 1932), 1, 20-21; *Mounds State Park Trail Map*, 1984, published and distributed by DNR; Marcia Smith Knowles, "Mounds State Park," *Indianapolis News*, 29 September 1992.

2. *Trail Map*; *Mound Builders*, 20-21; Kate Milner Rabb, "Mounds Park at Anderson Presented Formally to State," *Indianapolis Star*, 8 October 1930.

3. Information found in RG4269, Box 40 "State Parks," Folder "Mounds—WPA Project#3591," SA; "Conservation Reports," 1930-1942, passim.

LINCOLN STATE PARK

(Established 1932)

Hoosiers have long staked a claim to Abraham Lincoln, since he spent his formative years in the forests of what became Spencer County. The exact placement of his boyhood dwelling was much disputed, for it was, after all, but a rude cabin that no one would have thought to preserve, although after the President's assassination photographers descended upon what was supposed to be the rickety remains of the Lincoln homestead. Even if it had been so, the cabin was apparently demolished in the 1870s as the town of Lincoln City grew around the site. But the land was rich with Lincoln relics. The grave of his mother, Nancy Hanks Lincoln, was identified in 1879, and Spencer County acquired a half acre of land around it, purchasing another sixteen acres in 1900. The county fenced the entire tract and constructed a wide drive with iron gates, effectively setting up a memorial, as increasing numbers of people were coming to visit the grave. Interest was growing in the cabin site as well, and in 1917 a group of elderly residents gathered in the schoolyard that had replaced the presumed Lincoln farmstead and, straining memories over forty years old, agreed upon a site, upon which the county promptly placed a stone marker.[1]

With the creation of the Department of Conservation in 1919, along with director Richard Lieber's own intense interest in history, the state became interested in preserving significant memorials. In 1925 the General Assembly authorized four historical monuments to be administered by the Division of Lands and Waters, among them the Nancy Hanks Lincoln Burial Grounds. Lieber actively sought a fitting formal monument to Lincoln through the Indiana Lincoln Union, formed in late 1926. Three years later, the state acquired the cabin site property and began to plan a substantial memorial. In order that it be properly set apart and the sanctity of the gravesite preserved, the state acquired considerable southward acreage in which to place picnic shelters, campgrounds, and other recreational facilities. Lincoln State Park, established in 1932, was intended as an adjunct to the memorial proper.[2]

Just in time to develop the brand new park, CCC Company 1543, comprised of veterans, set up Camp SP-2 south of the highway (the present SR162

Stone marker erected in 1917 at the site where the Lincoln family cabin was believed to have been.

collection of GJ Greiff

88

runs through the former camp site) in the summer of 1933. In less than a year, the men completed Lincoln State Park's initial master plan, including a fire tower, an earth-fill dam impounding a thirty-acre lake, a lakeside shelter, and a ranger's cabin, which today is used for boat rentals. The CCC was busy on the north side of the highway as well, clearing the memorial site, grading, and planting trees. In the process some workers unearthed hearthstones believed to be part of the Lincoln cabin. Ironically, the cabin site memorial, finally dedicated in 1935, was a full-sized bronze casting by Thomas Hibben of the sill logs and hearth. The CCC company moved on to Turkey Run in the summer of 1934, and Federal Emergency Relief Administration workers graded and seeded their camp site and converted part of it into a recreation field. Meanwhile, the Department set up another FERA project to build fish rearing ponds below the dam in order to stock the lake. The WPA completed the work, constructed several miles of hiking trails, and built a large service building using salvaged lumber from the CCC camp. Later WPA workers built a gatehouse and a new entrance road. The remodeled park officially opened in 1938.[3]

The CCC originally built this for use as a ranger's cabin in 1934.
photo by GJ Greiff

In 1940 CCC Camp SP-15 was established for Company 553 to work on Lincoln State Park's ambitious new master plan that revolved around raising the earlier dam in order to enlarge the lake to about eighty acres, upon which would be a beach and a bath house pavilion similar to one already begun at Shakamak. A picnic area was to be developed along the north shoreline; on the south side plans called for a group camp. A custodian's cottage was also on the list. The CCC boys forged ahead and began nearly all the major projects at once, putting the park in "a torn up condition," which proved to be a mistake. The company was undermanned to begin with, and the impending World War II opened high-paying job possibilities for the young men, not to mention military service. The Department hastily regrouped and set the boys to work to complete the dam and the superintendent's residence. Park employees with some hired help managed to finish the latter after the camp closed in early 1942; in 1943 the General Assembly authorized sufficient funds to complete the abandoned dam project. Across the highway, the memorial buildings were erected, graced with the impressive limestone relief panels of sculptor E.H. Daniels, and the site was essentially complete by 1944.[4]

In the years after the war, people began to discover Lincoln State Park. The Division drew up a plan for a new group camp southwest of the lake, opened in 1956, the same year a new bath house was completed. The mystique of the adjacent memorial combined with the rise in family camping in general supported the Division's request for funds to build a large modern campground.[5]

In 1959 the National Park Service began investigating the possibility of establishing a national monument at the memorial site, although the area had already been designated a National Historic Site under the federal Historic Sites Act of 1935. But this would go further and place the property under the jurisdiction of NPS. In the summer of 1962, the memorial buildings, burial ground, and cabin site, totaling 115 acres, all became part of the Lincoln Boyhood National Memorial. SR162 was rerouted a bit to the south to incorporate all the buildings and to act as a boundary between the state and federal lands. This required a new gatehouse for the park, which was completed in 1964 along with ten family housekeeping cabins to add to the overnight accommodations. Not a great deal of additional development took place in Lincoln State Park for several years after, despite a new master plan devised in 1969. That plan mentioned an outdoor amphitheater. In 1984 the Division began a series of meetings with the Lincoln Drama Committee, with the idea of creating a summer-long run of an original musical play dramatizing the boyhood of Abraham Lincoln. In June 1987 a 1500-seat covered amphitheater opened on the west side of the park for the premier of *Young Abe Lincoln*, which continued annually for several summers under the auspices of the University of Southern Indiana. People came in droves and filled area motels as well as the park facilities, even on weekdays. The performances stopped in 2005, but in honor of Lincoln's 200th birthday, a brand new production combining live performance with multi-media debuted in June 2009.[6]

In 1991 the recently restored Colonel Jones House, less than three miles to the west at Gentryville, became a State Historic Site. Today it is administered as part of Lincoln State Park. William Jones (1803-1864) was a storekeeper for whom Lincoln had worked doing odd jobs and clerking in the store that once stood across the road. Jones thought highly of his young employee, allowing Lincoln access to all the books in his library. Although this house was built in 1834 after Lincoln left the state, the future President did spend the night in it during a campaign tour in 1844 for Whig presidential candidate Henry Clay.

The Lakeside Shelter was constructed by CCC Company 1543, comprised of World War I veterans.

photo by GJ Greiff

Jones himself was involved in politics and served in the Indiana legislature for four years. After the outbreak of the Civil War, Jones—although he was nearly sixty— joined the 53rd Regiment, Indiana Volunteers. He died in the Battle of Atlanta in July 1864. The house, listed in the National Register of Historic Places, is a one-story Greek Revival style dwelling with an uncharacteristic observation platform perched on top. It is open selected hours for self-guided tours and is frequently the site of special events.

The celebration of the bicentennial of Lincoln's birth in 2008-2010 stimulated even greater interest in our sixteenth President. The Indiana Abraham Lincoln Bicentennial Commission granted funds to a Fort Wayne sculptor, Will Clark, and an architect, George Morrison, from the same city, to create a public art plaza in Lincoln State Park in 2009. The large circular paved space in the Oak Grove area contains limestone pedestals commemorating key events in Lincoln's boyhood years in Indiana and a heroic bronze bust of the President. For perhaps a less structured approach, there is still the trail known as "Mr. Lincoln's Neighborhood Walk," which passes several sites significant to his boyhood as well as the grave of his sister Sarah.[7]

If one simply desires places of contemplation, the Sarah Lincoln Woods Nature Preserve beckons. Quieter times are possible in the fall, when the woods are lovely and southern Indiana weather tends to be at its best.[8]

 NOTES

1. See Jill York O'Bright, *"There I Grew Up . . .": A History of the Administration of Abraham Lincoln's Boyhood Home* (National Park Service study, 1987), 5-17.

2. "Conservation Reports," 1925, 324; 1927, 557-558; 1930, 545; 1931, 882; 1932, 366, 379; William E. Bartelt, "The Cabin Site Memorial and Its Architect," (Research Proposal for Lincoln Boyhood National Memorial, 1991), 3-4.

3. Information found in RG35, E115 "Camp Inspection Reports," Box 71, Indiana SP-2, NA; "Conservation Reports," 1934-1938, passim; Bartelt, "The Cabin Site Memorial," 8. See Greiff, 74-005 Cabin Site Memorial, SOS! File, HLFI.

4. RG35, E115 "Camp Inspection Reports," Box 72, Ind SP-15, NA; "Conservation Reports," 1941-1942, passim; "Southern-most State Park and Memorial Attracts Thousands," *Outdoor Indiana* 16 (July 1949), 10-11. See Greiff, 74-004 Lincoln Sculptured Panels, SOS! File, HLFI.

5. "Conservation Reports," 1956, 3, 20-21.

6. Interview, Daniel W. Bortner, Director of State Parks and Reservoirs, 30 June 2008.

7. "Fort Wayne Team Selected to Create Public Art Commemorating Abraham Lincoln's 200th Birthday," *Art's Eye*, Indiana Arts Commission online newsletter May 2008.

8. Information on development from "Conservation Reports," 1962, 6; 1964, 15; "DNR Reports," 1984, 213; 1986, 7, 19.

TIPPECANOE RIVER STATE PARK
(Established 1943)

In 1934 Congress authorized a New Deal program designed to put submarginal agricultural lands to use as recreational areas for families of limited means. Ideally such sites would be reasonably accessible to urban areas, whose residents were particularly in need of a place of escape. In early 1935 representatives of the Department of the Interior began to buy up property in Pulaski County north of Winamac along the Tippecanoe River and extending west across the state highway (present US35). It was not too difficult for the federal government to acquire the acreage, as much of it was in the hands of local banks or insurance companies. The land comprising the foreclosed farms and the few that were still solvent was sandy, swampy, and never very productive even in its early years of cultivation. A little over a hundred years before, bands of Potawatomi still roamed the area, where the floodplain yielded plentiful game and fish in the fall and winter.[1]

By November 1935 the newly established WPA began employing local men to develop the Winamac Recreation Demonstration Area. After cleaning out the scrub and beginning reforestation, the men set to work building a road to a new picnic area with a shelter house on the banks of the river, and two separate group camps. Even before the park was opened, the Boy Scouts made plans to use the camping facilities that summer. They were not disappointed, for the main buildings and most of the sleeping cabins of the first group camp were ready by June 1936. As was typical of the time, workers created a swimming beach on the river. By late 1938 the WPA had completed both camps, named Tepicon (which was occupied by the Girls Scouts) and Pottawattomie [sic], and most of the other recreational facilities, all of which were east of the highway. By the time the Indiana Department of Conservation accepted the land from the National Park Service in 1943, it was a complete state park with drives, trails, a campground, a

The WPA constructed this fire tower in the 1930s.

photo by GJ Greiff

92

picnic area, a fire tower overlooking the rapidly growing pine woods, and the two group camps. All remain, except Camp Tepicon, nearly all of which was torn down in the 1970s.[2] The name of the surviving group camp is today spelled "Potawatomi." Tepicon Hall, originally the dining hall for Camp Tepicon, still stands and is often used for retreats and reunions. It is listed in the National Register of Historic Places.[3]

When the state acquired the over six thousand acres that it renamed for the river that formed the park's eastern boundary, the Division waxed enthusiastically about further development projects, most of which did not materialize. In 1950, the park constructed a swimming pool to serve the two group camps, since the State Board of Health had declared swimming in the river to be "unsuitable." The park's marshy topography bred swarms of mosquitoes, which throughout the 1950s the Department attempted to control using DDT. The group camps, despite the insects, were extremely popular, and the park winterized the cabins for virtually year-round use.[4]

Tepicon Hall, built by the Works Progress Administration, is listed in the National Register of Historic Places.

photo by GJ Greiff

No recreational facilities existed on the property west of US35, and in the 1950s it was used as a Field Trial Area for dog fanciers. The Department determined that this section of the park might better serve the public under another division, and so over four thousand acres west of the highway became Winamac Fish and Game Area (today, Fish and Wildlife Area) in 1959. Only five miles to the north, Bass Lake State Beach came under Tippecanoe's administration in 1971 as an economy measure. Since Tippecanoe is one of the few state parks that does not offer public swimming (the pool is for group camp use), it was a happy arrangement. One admission fee covered both properties, until the Bass Lake parcel was turned over to the county in 2002.[5]

A fitting project, useful in interpreting Tippecanoe's natural history, is the twenty-acre waterfowl refuge completed in the mid-1970s south of the campground and picnic areas. It is a fine place for contemplation. The park offers long, winding foot and horse trails that are especially lovely in fall with the presence of so many mellow-toned oaks. Spring, too, is beautiful at Tippecanoe, but the hiker must be wary of sinking in the mud amidst the oxbows and freshets of the flood plain. The sight of masses of woodland flowers is likely worth the risk. The river can be deceptive; one visit may find it silent and sluggish, while the next time the Tippecanoe may have asserted itself upon all its old territory, reclaiming picnic grounds and inundating bridges.

1. See "Plans Afoot for 8,000-Acre Park on Tippecanoe," *Pulaski County (Winamac) Democrat*, 21 February 1935; John S. Bergman, *Tippecanoe River State Park* 45 (April 1980), 16.

2. Information on early development of Winamac RDA from RG79, E47 "Recreation Demonstration Areas," Box 150 (Project Reports 1936), NA; and R4269, Box 40 "State Parks," Folder "Winamac Recreation Demonstration Area, SA. See "Park-Forest Project Gets Federal Approval," *Pulaski County Democrat*, 1 August 1935; "See Early Start on Park Project," *Pulaski County Democrat*, 21 November 1935; "Work Under Way on Federal Park," *Pulaski County Democrat* 28 November 1935; "Work for 170 at Federal Park," *Pulaski County Democrat*, 2 January 1936; "Winamac," *Logansport Pharos-Tribune* 4 June 1936; "Scenes from New Winamac Park," *Pulaski County Democrat*, 20 August 1936; "Park Facilities Offered Groups for Short Camps," *Pulaski County Democrat*, 10 November 1938; "Expect Thousands at Camp Opening," *Pulaski County Democrat* 25 May 1939; "Tippecanoe River State Park Extends Recreational Facilities for Hoosiers," *Outdoor Indiana* 10 (July 1943), 8-9. "DNR Report," 1979, 142.

3　The name "Tepicon" (of which "Tippecanoe" is a variant), refers to a clan of the Miami and to an eighteenth century Miami village once located on the upper Tippecanoe River. See, for example, Richard White, *The Middle Ground: Indians, Empires, and Republics in the Great Lakes Region, 1650-1815*. New York: Cambridge University Press, 1991.

4. See "Conservation Reports," 1950, 621; 1951, 13; 1953, 14, 32.

5. See Bergman, "Tippecanoe," 17; *Tippecanoe River State Park Trail Map*, 1988, published and distributed by DNR. "DNR Report," 1972, 78.

VERSAILLES STATE PARK
(Established 1943)

During the New Deal when Congress passed a law authorizing federal Recreation Demonstration Areas on land unsuitable for farming, among the earliest projects the planners agreed upon was that near the town of Versailles. The area along winding Laughery Creek both north and south of US50 was mostly wooded, rugged and rocky, proven nearly impossible for agriculture by the nineteenth century farmers who tried, but very well suited for outdoor recreation. Acquisition began in the fall of 1934, and local workers hired through FERA soon began building an access road and a group camp overlooking the creek. The following January it became Indiana CCC Camp NP-1, occupied by Company 596, which set to work on the basic infrastructure, picnic areas, and a campground. FERA, soon supplanted by the WPA, also continued to administer work projects in the new park, giving employment to scores of men from the region.[1]

The area had first been considered for a state park in the early 1920s, when businessman Joseph Hassmer, a former resident, offered a large tract of land on Laughery Creek north of the town, along with a contribution of funds to develop it. After federal work on the RDA began in 1935, Hassmer donated a 65-acre parcel called Hassmer Hill, which included a large house, in order that a regional 4-H camp might be built there. The federal government accepted the offer, and both the CCC and the WPA workers hurried to complete the new camp in time for its first group of 4-Hers in July 1936. Over the next forty years, other organizations, including school groups, used the Hassmer Hill camp, but its primary association was with 4-H. Members from fourteen counties in the region enjoyed the camp's rustic facilities—as well as its swimming pool—but DNR discontinued the camp in 1977 and demolished all the buildings. (The house had burned in 1955.) By that time most of the structures needed substantial repair, and besides, flooding the new Versailles Lake had left Hassmer Hill indeed high and dry, with no access from the main part of the park.[2]

In 1943 the National Park Service turned over Winamac and Versailles, its two Recreation Demonstration Areas in Indiana, to the state. Versailles comprised over five thousand acres, on which the Department of Conservation received a ready-made park with an improved campground, a picnic grove complete with an attractive shelter house, seven miles of hiking trails, a fire tower, and two group camps (Hassmer Hill and the one the CCC had occupied, now called Camp Laughery). But other

Nestled in an oak grove, this beautiful shelterhouse was built in the 1930s.   *photo by GJ Greiff*

95

than at the Hassmer Hill camp, there were no swimming facilities. As early as 1948 the Department began to buy up land in order to impound a lake in the Laughery Creek valley, but the project became entangled in lawsuits for the next five years. Work began at last in 1954, with some labor provided by an Honor Camp administered through the Department of Correction. By 1956 the dam was completed and work begun on a beach and bath house, opened for the summer of 1958.[3]

In addition to the 230-acre lake, the Division had once beheld grandiose visions of building up to three more group camps and a park inn, as well as either converting or constructing new family cabins. But none of these came to fruition. The park did build a saddle barn in 1960, a new gatehouse and another campground in the 1970s, but the lake remained the park's most significant addition, at least until, ironically, an Olympic-size pool was opened in 1987. The beach on the lovely water set amidst the rocky hills closed, although fishing and boating continue to draw visitors to the lake.[4]

At the entrance to the park is a covered bridge built in 1885 by Thomas A. Hardman on what was once the old road to Cincinnati, precursor to the present US50 just to the south. The Busching (some sources call it Bushing) Bridge is over 170 feet long and was restored by the county in 2005. The rocky terrain and mature oak forests of Versailles make for soul-stirring hikes up and down the ravines, particularly in spring and fall. The park's Oak Grove is, in fact, largely infiltrated with maples that create a spectacular autumn display, especially when accompanied by the constant rustle of the leaves dancing at one's feet.

 NOTES

1. Information on development found in RG79, E47, "Recreation Demonstration Areas," Box 150 (correspondence, press releases, 1934-1935), NA.

2. "Proposes $25,000 Gift for a New State Park," *Indianapolis News*, 8 October 1921; John Murphy, "Versailles Camp to Offer Low Wage Groups Advantages of State Resorts," *Indianapolis Times* 24 March 1936; "The Development of Hassmer Hill 4-H Camp," *Versailles Republican*, 19 August 1993.

3. "State Accepts Two Park Areas," *Indianapolis News*, 29 April 1943; "Versailles State Park in Ripley County Has Scenic Setting Among Wooded Hills," *Outdoor Indiana* 20 (June 1943), 6-7; Information on postwar development from "Conservation Reports," 1949, 277; 1950, 622; 1957, 33; 1958, 1, 50; Victor Peterson, "Expect Work to Begin Next Spring on New Versailles Park Lake," *Indianapolis Times*, 26 July 1948; "Fund for Versailles Lake," *Indianapolis Star* 9 July 1954.

4. *General Plan for the Future Development of Versailles State Park* (Indianapolis: Department of Conservation, 1944); "Conservation Report," 1960, I-60; "DNR Reports," 1972, 78; 1975, 106; 1987, 5.

SHADES STATE PARK
(Established 1947)

Similar in topography to Turkey Run but with more spectacular views of Sugar Creek and the surrounding woodland, the area first known locally as "The Shades of Death" had been a popular private resort since the 1880s. Earlier, Piankeshaw Indians, a clan of the Miami tribe, had lived amidst the deeply forested canyons and ridges. The mineral springs in the area had long drawn early travelers, who marveled at the fancifully eroded sandstone that called up such names as the Devil's Punch Bowl and Devil's Backbone. In the 1880s a small corporation, the Garland Dells Mineral Springs Association, purchased the three springs and about three hundred surrounding acres. Over time they built a large frame hotel and additional accommodations in cabins, cottages, and tents with wooden floors, all of which could house a total of about two hundred people. Served by weekly excursions via the Midland Railroad through nearby Waveland, the resort was very popular. State geologist Edward Barrett in 1917 called the Shades "perhaps the most beautiful and picturesque region carved in the Mansfield sandstone," out of an area covering parts of fifteen counties.[1]

In 1909 Joseph W. Frisz, the "Father of Shades," had purchased with several partners stock in the resort corporation; a few years later he achieved full control. Over the next twenty-odd years until his death in 1939, Frisz not only zealously protected the canyons, ravines, and forests of the original tract but added over two thousand acres to the property. While the resort offered more sophisticated amusements in its large pavilion, such as dances, motion pictures, and concerts, these types of activities were restricted to a small area, and brochures touted The Shades as a "scenic park," the "Yosemite of Indiana."[2]

The Civilian Conservation Corps in 1935 established a camp at the Shades, largely owing to Mr. Frisz's generosity in giving the government a free lease on the land. Camp SCS-3 was not a state park camp; rather, it worked under the auspices of the U.S. Department of Agriculture. The boys of CCC Company 2579, which occupied the facility, engaged in soil conservation and erosion control projects on farms throughout four counties. They did no work on the resort property.[3]

It was no surprise that timber companies panted eagerly to buy the property when Frisz's heirs decided to sell in 1947. Fortunately the beauty of the Shades was so widely known that individuals and organizations immediately responded to the Department of Conservation's unprecedented cry for help. An Indianapolis businessman, Arthur W. Baxter, formed a holding company to purchase the property until public subscription could raise enough funds, which was soon

"THE SHADES," INDIANA'S MOST PICTURESQUE SUMMER RESORT.

PAVILION AND ENTRANCE.

Little evidence remains today of the park's colorful past as a private resort.

collection of Tom Hohman

97

A Side View of Bridal Veil Falls

Bridal Veil Falls has changed little from this 1920s view.   *collection of GJ Greiff*

accomplished. Indiana's conservation clubs, particularly, were involved in collecting sums large and small at the grass roots level to help acquire the state's fifteenth park.[4] After accepting the property, the Department kept the hotel operating as a park inn for several years, but upkeep was too costly to warrant continuing the operation, and after briefly serving as a group camp in the mid-1960s, the building was demolished. The nearby pavilion, the last remnant of the old resort, was torn down in 1980; the site is now a picnic grove. One odd feature at Shades that many considered intrusive was the Roscoe Turner Flight Strip constructed in 1960, complete with a pilots' lounge (razed long ago). It had been a pet project of Department of Conservation head Kenneth Marlin, himself a pilot, who managed to get a turf landing field leveled with the aid of personnel from the Division of Fish and Game. Asserting that airplanes were not compatible with wildlife, state parks director Kenneth R. Cougill had been against the idea, even attempting to enlist the aid of the National Park Service and the National Conference on State Parks. Despite that and ripples of public protest, the landing field went through.[5] Rarely used, the air strip for years appeared to be simply an open grassy area, and it disappeared from park maps in the 2000s.

Shades remains among the least developed of Indiana's state parks offering only the most traditional pursuits of hiking, picnicking, camping and fishing. At the eastern part of the property is Pine Hills, Indiana's first nature preserve, dedicated in 1968. Although the park seems especially well suited for long communes with nature, summer weekends tend to find Shades crowded and noisy. Choose late fall or early spring for clambering up and down challenging trails that provide beautiful vistas from 210 feet above Sugar Creek and delightful encounters with wildlife. Despite the historic names conjuring up the devil, a hiker will likely find spiritual inspiration from an entirely different direction amidst the rugged terrain.

Views of beautiful Sugar Creek add to the wonder of the rugged hiking trails in the park.

photo by GJ Greiff

98

1. Edward Barrett, *41st Annual Report of Department of Geology and Natural Resources* (Fort Wayne: Fort Wayne Printing Company 1917), 81; see "The Springs at the Shades," *Outdoor Indiana* 16 (April 1949), 14; *Shades State Park Trail Map* (1981) published and distributed by DNR.

2. See "Nature Created a Real Conservationist Who Loved and Preserved the 'Shades of Death'," *Outdoor Indiana* 9 (December 1942), 7, 15. Several brochures ca. 1920s-1930s advertising The Shades and the Shades Hotel are in the State Parks Clippings Files, "Shades" folder, ISL.

3. *Indiana District, Civilian Conservation Corps: 1938-1939,* 128-131; see Karen Zach, "Civilian Conservation Corps Tied to Waveland," *Montgomery Magazine* (May 1992) 3-4.

4. "Save the Shades," brochure published by the Indiana Department of Conservation, 1947; "Conservation Clubs Play Big Role in Drive to Create Park," *Outdoor Indiana* (December 1947), 7; "Conservation Reports," 1947, 673, 1948, 809.

5. "DNR Reports," 1965, 23, 25; 1970, 4; 1981, 177; Interview, Hasenstab, 23 May 1995.

WHITEWATER MEMORIAL STATE PARK

(Established 1949)

Perhaps the mark of a true state park rests on whether it includes a communing place, a space in which one may sit in reverie, in solitude amidst "nature"—hard to come by, in these times, even in the largest parks. Whitewater, which is by design and usage a family-oriented recreational park, nonetheless does meet the criterion with its small Hornbeam Nature Preserve on the southwest side of Whitewater Lake. Named for the abundance of hornbeam trees, the preserve is a relatively old and undisturbed beech-maple forest covering steep hills and ravines. Some of the stream beds reveal fossils—or what appear to be fossils in the making, layers of shells or their impressions that have only barely become rock. The fairly abundant understory suggests deer are not as much of a problem in this park as in others, but in any case they might prefer foraging in the adjacent farmland.

Although Whitewater became a state park in 1949, there is still something of a "new" look about it (unlike its similar counterpart Shakamak, which is twenty years older). Located in the Whitewater River valley, the rolling terrain interlaced with patches of forests and farmland was acquired through the efforts of four counties: Fayette, Franklin, Wayne, and Union. Noting an obvious demand for a state-run recreational facility in eastern Indiana, in 1943 the legislature had adopted a resolution authorizing a survey of the Whitewater valley in hopes of finding a suitable site for a state park.[1] The residents of the four counties, united through the Whitewater Memorial Park Association, Inc., began in 1945 to raise funds to purchase approximately 1800 acres along Silver Creek south of Liberty, a site approved by the Department of Conservation. Local conservation clubs promoted the park heavily, which from the start was intended also as a memorial— a "living tribute"—to the counties' war dead. Four years later the state took formal possession of 1512 acres with a dedication ceremony sparked with patriotic fervor at the site of the dam yet to be constructed on Silver Creek. It would create the park's main attraction, a lake of nearly two hundred acres, which was opened in 1953.[2]

Fossils not fully hardened lie along the trail through the Hornbeam Nature Preserve.

photo by GJ Greiff

Swimming, fishing, and boating are still the primary lures of Whitewater, along with heavily used picnic grounds, family cabins, campgrounds, and a saddle barn. Forest cover has grown sufficiently to provide shady groves overlooking the lake. Although early Conservation Department reports noted the historical significance of the region both as an area of early territorial settlement starting around 1806 and its importance as a favored hunting ground for native Americans—chiefly Delaware (Lenape)—prior to that, little of this is interpreted to the public.

Opportunities to gaze at the water and throw in a fishing line abound in the park.

photo by GJ Greiff

 **NOTES**

1. "Whitewater Valley Survey Is Made by Conservation Group." Press release, 22 May 1944, from Indiana Department of Conservation.

2. See "Proposed Site for New State Park Selected," *Indianapolis Star*, 21 December 1944; "Meet the Whitewater Memorial Park," *Outdoor Indiana* 12 (July 1945), 5, 14; "Whitewater Memorial—Newest State Park!" *Outdoor Indiana* 16 (January 1949), 6-7; "Whitewater Memorial Park—Indiana's 16th—Is Dedicated," *Outdoor Indiana* 16 (September 1949), 2; "Whitewater Memorial State Park Soon a Reality," *Outdoor Indiana* 18 (January 1951), 12-13.

CHAIN O'LAKES STATE PARK
(Dedicated 1960)

Not unnoted by citizens and administrators alike was the relative scarcity of state parks in the northern half of the state. Among the region's most typical features are the rolling moraine landscape and gravel-bottomed kettle lakes formed by the last of the receding glaciers some thirteen thousand years ago. The possibility of the state's securing a connected chain of several such lakes in the vicinity of Lagrange arose as early as the late 1930s. By mid-1946, interest had settled on a series of nine small, relatively unspoiled lakes, eight of which were linked to one another, south of Albion in Noble County for a proposed "Chain-of-Lakes" State Park.[1]

Originally the plan was for an ad hoc association of the four counties most closely concerned—Allen, Dekalb, Whitley, and Noble—to find a means to raise funds to buy some 2700 acres surrounding the lakes and then present the land to the state. A multi-county fund drive in the late 1940s had led to the acquisition of Whitewater Memorial State Park in Union County, but the counties hoping to establish Chain O'Lakes chose instead to levy a local tax to purchase the site. Opposition soon developed in the three less populous counties—Dekalb County never did join the rest—resulting in a citizen's lawsuit filed in 1949 that challenged the legality of the tax. With the dismissal of the suit nearly six years later, the Tri-County Park Board (Allen, Whitley, Noble) acquired about eight hundred acres; in 1959 the General Assembly approved the funds needed to buy the

Toward sunset the boats are all in and Miller Lake is a peaceful sight.

photo by GJ Greiff

remaining necessary tracts to total two thousand acres. By the time Governor Harold Handley officially dedicated Chain O'Lakes as Indiana's twentieth state park in June 1960, fifteen hundred acres were in state hands and the rest shortly followed. Ultimately eleven lakes were included within park boundaries. Chain O'Lakes opened with only a beach on Sand Lake, the largest, and some limited camping facilities.[2]

Initially, the lack of development around the lakes, nestled amidst cultivated farmland, orchards, and woodlots, inspired the notion of a park devoted to hiking and camping and quiet pursuits of nature. It has become over the years a family-oriented park whose visitors tend toward active outdoor recreation in and on the water.

Chain O'Lakes State Park revels in both its ancient glacial and its recent agrarian pasts. In between, the area was home to a tribe of native Americans, the Miami. The park's nature center is housed in an adapted one-room school built in

1915. Students attended the Stanley School into the 1950s. Farmland has surrendered to tapestried fields of wildflowers, while old orchards, still readily visible, now compete with scrub trees and the harbingers of a forest. The dedicated above-ground archaeologist may stumble upon the sites of farmyards and barn lots, even though the buildings are all gone. The park offers a surprisingly diverse landscape to those who seek contemplative spots.

Yarrow is among the many wildflowers that now thrive where once fields of corn and soybeans grew.

photo by GJ Greiff

 NOTES

1. "Upstate Lakes Sought for Park," *The Indianapolis News*, 19 October 1945; "Gates, Officials of 4 Counties to Discuss Financing of New Chain-of-Lakes Park," *The Indianapolis Star*, 9 July 1946; "Conservation Report," 1960, I-14.

2. Conservation Report," 1960, I-13 through I-15; "Noble County Park Suit is Dropped," *Indianapolis News*, 6 June 1955; Pat Redmond, "Chain-O-Lakes Couldn't Help Becoming Park," *Indianapolis News*, 15 April 1960.

OUABACHE STATE PARK

(Established 1962)

Despite the best efforts of the state to educate the public that the park was named for the Wabash River that flows beside it and is merely the French spelling of the same word, mispronunciation persists. "Oo-BA-chee" is still widely used. The idea was to acknowledge the influence of the Jesuit "black robe" missionaries that early had sought to convert the native Americans in this part of Indiana. Miami had settled in small villages on both sides of the river, but by 1829 the first white settler erected a cabin in the vicinity, and the removal of the tribes followed over the next two decades. Pioneer farmers soon cleared the land, which became part of Wells County.[1]

A century later, much of the farmland had played out. The Wells County State Forest and Game Preserve was established on a largely eroded, scrubby parcel near Bluffton in 1935, administered jointly by the divisions of Forestry and of Fish and Game. Conservation practice in the 1930s leaned toward a policy of managed wildlife distribution and the propagation of game birds for release in the wild. With the goal of building a state-of-the-art game farm that focused on raising quail, the Department of Conservation immediately set up CCC Camp S-93. The young men of Company 1592 began work that summer and continued through 1940, constructing bird pens, hatcheries and other buildings for propagation, as well as various recreational structures for public use. The WPA also worked extensively on the property. The Department encouraged Hoosiers to visit the game farm; as was typical in the 1930s, it offered numerous educational displays and live animal exhibits among the sights. After the CCC vacated the property shortly before World War II, conscientious objectors engaged in public service projects occupied the camp buildings, which were torn down for salvage materials a few years later.[2]

When trends in conservation led to abandoning the artificial propagation of game birds (especially non-native varieties) in the early 1960s, the future of Wells County State Game Preserve was in doubt. As the property already contained recreational structures, a transfer from the Division of Fish and Game to the Division of State Parks seemed a wise move. No doubt the serendipity of an already-developed park facility within twenty miles of Fort Wayne was obvious. The land became Indiana's twenty-second state park (the state has since discontinued some) in 1962, and for about twenty years was called Ouabache State Recreation Area.[3] This was an attempt at the time to distinguish the more "pristine" parks from those areas that

1945

PHEASANT BROODER HOUSE, RACOON AND ANIMAL DISPLAY BUILDINGS AT STATE PARK, BLUFFTON, IND. L-61A

Breeding and display facilities at Wells County State Forest and Game Preserve.

collection of Tom Hohman

104

were established primarily for recreation and needed to be "naturalized" into a more forested state. The CCC's earliest plantings of trees on the property were just starting to mature. The Department did not need to do much in the way of additional recreational development at first, since there were numerous picnic areas, shelterhouses, hiking trails, and campgrounds already in place, as well as a sizable manmade lake for fishing. But most of the game farm facilities needed to be removed, although the Department adapted some of the buildings for park use. The game preserve had not charged admission, so a gatehouse was an immediate need. By the 1970s, a master plan at hand, the park undertook further development, most notably an Olympic-size swimming pool and of course, more improved campgrounds. Its past associations were not forgotten, however; work included the construction of a new twenty-acre pen for large animals.[4] Once an important feature at several of the state parks, the exhibit of live bison at Ouabache is the last one remaining to help interpret Indiana's natural history to the public.

Pine plantations of the 1930s along with some older stands of oak and hickory offer pleasant hiking through the woods for those who prefer contemplative walks. Late fall is often the best time to appreciate the effect of decades of planned "naturalization" on this formerly eroded land.

Lodge built by the CCC for the Wells County State Forest and Game Preserve.
photo by GJ Greiff

 NOTES

1. See Bob Greiner, "Coming of Age," *Outdoor Indiana* 54 (May 1989), 20; *Ouabache State Recreation Area Trail Map*, ca. 1980, published and distributed by DNR.

2. RG 79, E115 "Camp Inspection Reports," Box 69, NA; "Conservation Reports," 1936, 432; 1941, 926; "CCC Camp Buildings in Wells County Razed for Salvage," *Fort Wayne Journal-Gazette*, 22 January 1944; Greiff, "Potential WPA Historic Properties in Indiana," 1988 (compilation prepared for and on file with HLFI).

3. See later chapter, "Former State Parks," for information on those properties that are no longer state parks.

4. "State to Get Ready-Made Park," *Indianapolis Times*. 28 December 1961, 19. "Conservation Report," 1962, 5; "DNR Report," 1975, 104. See Greiner, "Coming of Age," 20.

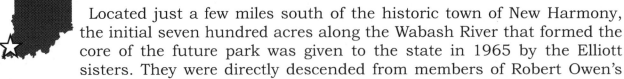

HARMONIE STATE PARK
(Dedicated 1978)

Located just a few miles south of the historic town of New Harmony, the initial seven hundred acres along the Wabash River that formed the core of the future park was given to the state in 1965 by the Elliott sisters. They were directly descended from members of Robert Owen's intellectual communal society upriver that flourished briefly during the mid-1820s. Owen had purchased the settlement site from the Rappites, who had founded it as Harmonie ten years earlier. The Elliotts' tract, offered in memory of their father, Elmer E. Elliott, had formed a part of the original Rappite holdings. As the sisters' donation lay within easy reach of the Evansville metropolitan area, it seemed an ideal site to develop into the state park that numerous studies had deemed was needed in the region.[1]

Although he had farmed much of the property for decades, Mr. Elliott, a dedicated conservationist, had planted extensive stands of timber in the hillier sections. He had even developed a modest resort area with ramshackle cabins, but the Department elected not to use them. The state immediately began to acquire adjacent land along the river for what was then called Harmonie State Recreation Area. The Division allowed people to use the property within a few years, and by the early 1970s had constructed service buildings and a primitive campground, along with some picnic areas. By 1978 the property had grown fivefold, and Governor Otis Bowen dedicated Harmonie State Park that August in a ceremony at the new Olympic-size swimming pool, which was named in honor of Elmer Elliott. Besides the pool, the new park offered modern and primitive camping, hiking trails, and picnic areas.[2] The park has since added attractive family housekeeping cabins built of logs and more picnic shelters. Some of the hiking trails follow old country lanes past former farmsites. Incredibly, when the park opened, there was no access to its most significant feature, the Wabash River—not even a hiking trail. In the 1980s

Family cabins at Harmonie are very popular.

photo by GJ Greiff

the Department set up the only place of encounter, a boat ramp and a picnic grove on a nearby bluff. Since the river is so much a part of Indiana song and story, one might hope for more opportunities.

Harmonie also contains oil wells and storage barrels—not unusual in this part of Indiana, but seldom found in state parks. Unused wells are being capped, and interpretive signage near the north end of the park now explains the somewhat disconcerting sight. The most developed area of Harmonie is the north

106

end where the entrance is located; farther south is a more mature woods laden with deer and trails especially lovely in the spring and fall.

The swimming pool is a welcome respite during humid southern Indiana summers.

photo by GJ Greiff

 NOTES

1. "Governor Branigan Releases Location of State Park," *The New Harmony Times*, 30 December 1965; Ron Wormald, "Sisters Donate 700 Acres of Land for State Park," *Evansville Courier*, 31 December 1965; "Frontage on Wabash Given for State Park," *Indianapolis Star*, 31 December 1965; Wayne Guthrie, "Elliott Park Proponents Active," *Indianapolis News*, 7 February 1966.

2. See "DNR Reports," 1973, 80; 1975, 101; 1979, 135; see also Wormald, "Sisters Donate 700 Acres"; "State Officials to Dedicate Newest State Park at Pool," *Indianapolis Star*, 6 August 1978; Myrtie Barker, "New State Park Has Historic Background," *Indianapolis News*, 6 September 1978.

POTATO CREEK STATE PARK

(Dedicated 1977)

Strictly in terms of usage, Potato Creek is one of Indiana's most popular parks, near to South Bend-Mishawaka and within range of the Calumet area. Camping and fishing are the most common pursuits.

The opportunity for quiet bonding with nature, however, can be minimal during much of the peak season. Despite the fact that northern Indiana abounds in glacier-formed lakes, the park's Worster Lake, over three hundred acres, is the result of impounding the waters of Potato Creek. Undeveloped natural lakes suitable for state park development were no longer available in the late 1960s when acquisition of the land began. The lake is named for the late Darcy Worster, a local man who, with many of his fellow conservation club members, had first dreamed of damming the creek to create a recreational reservoir in the 1930s.[1]

The Vollmer Report, a master plan for Indiana's state parks completed in 1964, identified the South Bend vicinity as one of five metropolitan areas in Indiana that lacked a state park conveniently close by. At one point a location north of the Indiana Toll Road was considered (it, too, had no natural lake), but the Potato Creek site won out over the vociferous protests of local landowners who were loath to give up their property. Once most of the park land was secured and the dam built, the public was allowed to come in for picnicking and hiking while the park was still its early stages of development.[2]

In the fall of 1977 Governor Otis Bowen officially opened and dedicated Potato Creek State Recreation Area. (At that time the Division was attempting to maintain a distinction between scenic parks and those developed for recreational use with minimal esthetic value.) Reforestation had only just begun; much of the area was open land. But modern family and horseman's campgrounds, youth tent camping, bicycle trails, boat rentals and a sizable beach awaited the new park's visitors. From the start, cross-country skiing has been available in winter.

The waters of Worster Lake in Potato Creek State Park bring peaceful thoughts toward sunset.

photo by GJ Greiff

Upon completion in 1982 of several more capital improvements, most notably new family cabins, Governor Robert Orr presided over another dedication ceremony for what was now called Potato Creek State Park.[3]

Although at first primarily a family recreational park, efforts began in the 1990s to restore some areas of the park to their original natural states of prairie and wetland, an effort that continues. The park has a full-time naturalist available. In keeping with the state parks' connection with history, the Porter-Rea Cemetery, with headstones dating back to the 1850s, is of interest. Here are buried side-by-side members of both Caucasian and African-American farm families, the earliest of the latter from the pre-Civil War Huggart Settlement. The cemetery, whose chartered association started in 1884, is still used. So that its agricultural use will not be forgotten, Cultural Arts projects using oral history interviews have attempted to document the history of farm life in the region.

Potato Creek offers something to the nature lover who appreciates a more subtle beauty. Its varied habitats are filled with birds and other wildlife. The Swamp Rose Nature Preserve, a natural wetland, lies in the northeast corner of the park. The Department is restoring another wetland of about eighty acres in the northwest corner of the park that was drained in the late nineteenth century.[4] That much of the property was cultivated into the 1960s remains obvious, but there is considerable beauty in the transitional vegetation.

 NOTES

1. Trail Map, Potato Creek State Recreation Area, published by DNR, 1980; Interview, Pagac.

2. Philip F. Clifford, "Park Opposition Plea Echoes Up a Creek," *Indianapolis Star*, 22 January 1967; "Upstate Park Land Buying to Start Soon," *Indianapolis Star*, 23 March 1968; *Trail Map*; "DNR Report," 1975, 104.

3. *Master Plan 1978+*, 27; "DNR Reports," 1983, 177; *Trail Map*.

4. Wayne Falda, "Nature's Own Restoration," *South Bend Tribune*, 5 October 1992.

SUMMIT LAKE STATE PARK
(Dedicated 1988)

The lake dominates this appropriately named state park northeast of New Castle; virtually all its recreational opportunities revolve around the body of water created by impounding the Big Blue River in 1982.

The Big Blue River Conservancy District, funded by the federal Soil Conservation Service (part of the Department of Agriculture), acquired the land and built the dam, opening the lake to the public in 1985. The project was intended as a reservoir for flood control and water supply, as well as to provide recreation. But the district, encompassing parts of Henry and Rush counties, was too small and sparsely populated to generate sufficient tax money to develop the property fully and maintain it. District officials then approached the state, which at first leased the property and finally arranged to purchase it when attendance quickly demonstrated the park's popularity. [1]

The region was certainly ripe for a state park. The Vollmer Plan—the master plan for Indiana state parks in the 1960s—had targeted the Muncie area as one that was lacking in sufficient outdoor recreational opportunities. In 1972 the Division of State Parks had acquired 850 acres just north of New Castle and immediately undertook to develop it as Wilbur Wright State Recreation Area. Within a year there were campsites and picnic areas completed, but late in 1973 the land was transferred to the Division of Fish and Wildlife, which manages the property today as Wilbur Wright Fish and Wildlife Area. [2] Fifteen more years passed before an actual state park in the region became a reality.

Anglers quickly discovered Summit Lake's charms. The family campgrounds are full most weekends, and the beach draws crowds throughout central Indiana's humid summers. Most of the park was farmed until shortly before its acquisition and so is largely open land, some of which is being reforested. But the property lies on the Mississippi flyway and has a wetland natural area tucked up in its northeast corner, as well as a small deciduous woods. Watchers of both waterfowl and songbirds find the park a paradise, as over a hundred different types of birds have been spotted within its confines. The once endangered Canada geese have become something of a problem and the Department is attempting to control the population. The grasslands—formerly cultivated fields—offer successive colorful carpets of wildflowers over the warm months.

Peaceful sunset in late fall over Summit Lake.

photo by GJ Greiff

Encounters with nature at Summit Lake tend to be subtle but occasionally spectacular, as the enthralling sight of a soaring bald eagle in late fall, or a multi-hued sunset over the water.[3]

Wildflowers flourish at Summit Lake.

photo by GJ Greiff

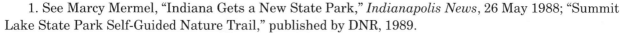 NOTES

1. See Marcy Mermel, "Indiana Gets a New State Park," *Indianapolis News*, 26 May 1988; "Summit Lake State Park Self-Guided Nature Trail," published by DNR, 1989.

2. "DNR Reports," 1972, 72, 78; 1973, 77, 83; 1974, 105.

3. Rita Rose, "Newest Park for Nature Lovers," *Indianapolis Star*, 10 July 1988; Donna L. Bonner, "Changing Seasons at Summit Lake State Park," *Outdoor Indiana* 59 (January/February 1994), 22-23; writer's fieldwork, 19 September 1992 and 13 June 1995.

THE FALLS OF THE OHIO STATE PARK
(Dedicated 1994)

While few would dispute the worthiness of the Falls of the Ohio to be preserved, many question its appellation as a state park. The realm of the Division of Museums and Memorials seems more appropriate, especially since the park's chief attraction, besides the Devonian fossil beds, is a wonderful museum opened in 1994 that interprets all aspects of the complex natural and human history pertaining to the immediate area. But the struggle to preserve the falls—more accurately a series of rapids caused by limestone outcroppings of ancient coral—was long and convoluted, involving years of interstate wranglings with Kentucky. After all was resolved in 1990, Indiana established the state park, with the prestige of that nomenclature befitting the site. With virtually no recreational facilities to offer, save for a discontiguous picnic area near the homesite of Revolutionary War hero George Rogers Clark, DNR proudly touted the park as a "nature and education center." In 2003, the park constructed a representation of the Clark cabin close to its original site, high on a bluff opposite Goose Island, with a splendid view of the river upstream and down. George Rogers Clark was the older brother of William Clark, who, with Meriwether Lewis and the Corps of Discovery, departed on their historic journey from Clarksville in October 1803. An interpreter staffs the cabin at certain times. Falls of the Ohio State Park today offers a variety of educational experiences.[1]

It was not always so. By the mid-twentieth century the fossil beds, much looted over the years, had become a toxic dumping ground, which, nevertheless, was home to an astonishing array of wildlife. Designated a National Natural Landmark in 1966, the Falls of the Ohio was declared, along with two nearby islands, a National Wildlife Conservation Area in 1982, of which the state park is a tiny part. Once the issue was settled, cleanup of the riverbank began, and the task took over a year before the

The recreated George Rogers Clark Cabin overlooking the Ohio River.
photo by GJ Greiff

groundbreaking in the fall of 1992. The stunning museum building appears to be an architectural interpretation of the geology of the Falls, perhaps suggesting as well the layers of knowledge within. Outside the Interpretive Center is a bronze statue of Lewis and Clark by Montana artist C. A. Grende, created in 2003 for the Bicentennial of their epic expedition that began from near this point.[2]

As for the world-renowned fossil beds, the vagaries of weather and the river frequently make them inaccessible. They are submerged when the river is high, and hiking amidst them in rain or winter conditions can be treacherous. Late summer or fall is the best time to see them. For all the cleanup that preceded the park's opening, receding high water continues to leave behind a disheartening mountain of trash, familiar to those who hike along rivers. Still, the sight of an ascending heron or the antics of a scurrying sandpiper—not to mention the stunning array of fossils—make it all worthwhile.

The unusual fossil beds at the Falls of the Ohio are a designated National Natural Landmark.

photo by GJ Greiff

 NOTES

1. Pat Ralston, Director of DNR, quoted in Tom Chiat, "Back from Extinction," *Indianapolis Star*, 13 March 1994. Interview, Pagac; *The Falls of the Ohio State Park* (park brochure distributed by DNR, 1993). Steve Knowles, Property Manager, Falls of the Ohio State Park, electronic mail message to author, 27 May 2003; interview with author on site, 29 May 2003.

2. *Ibid.*; "DNR Report," 1966, 25; see "Falls of the Ohio: The First Neighborhood," *Discover Louisville* (Louisville: Louisville Historical League, 1986), 6-15; Greiff, *Remembrance, Faith, and Fancy: Outdoor Public Sculpture in Indiana* (Indianapolis: Indiana Historical Society, 2005).

CHARLESTOWN STATE PARK

(Established 1996)

As World War II loomed on the horizon, the federal government searched for a relatively isolated location on which to establish a facility for the manufacture of munitions. Adjacent to the Ohio River near historic Charlestown, founded in 1808, and well served by railroads, were several thousand acres of agricultural land and woods surrounding the rugged valley of Fourteenmile Creek. There had been a mill on the creek even before the town was platted, and Charlestown served as the seat of Clark County for much of the nineteenth century. The town had settled into a quiet existence as an agricultural center with a population of only about 900 when the federal government came to buy up the adjacent farmland. In a few years, it had swollen to over 13,000. Established in 1940, the Indiana Army Ammunition Plant ultimately totaled about fifteen thousand acres, much of it buffering the actual munitions factory, a vast complex that during World War II employed thousands in the manufacture of smokeless powder. But as the decades passed, the federal government at last abandoned the largely unused facility in the early 1990s, officially closing it in 1995.[1]

While much of the property was occupied by endless acres of industrial buildings, the unglaciated valley of Fourteenmile Creek and the area immediately surrounding it had lain virtually untouched for nearly fifty years. It was this section of the former munitions plant that the state acquired in parcels totaling over two thousand acres. Charlestown State Park officially opened in 1996, offering fishing opportunities, picnic spots, and hiking trails; a campground followed a few years later. Another acquisition through a transfer of ownership from the United States Army doubled the park in 2004 and provided opportunities to develop access to the Ohio River. The first project was a boat ramp, completed in 2007, with an overlook from which to contemplate the river just downstream. While the park is much used locally—the large metropolitan area of Jeffersonville and New Albany lies less than twenty miles away—Charlestown offers wonderful opportunities to have quiet and close encounters with nature. The mix of open areas, underbrush, and deep woods encourage a great variety of wildlife, from wild turkeys, quail, and ubiquitous rabbits to snakes, bats, and hawks.[2]

Starting in the 1880s a recreational area called Fern Grove between the Ohio River and a bend of Fourteenmile Creek near its mouth was a popular destination for church picnics and family gatherings. Louisville entrepreneur David Rose bought the resort in 1923 and turned it into a popular amusement park called Rose

The Fern Cliff Hotel provided overnight accommodations for those seeking relaxation at the Fern Grove resort.

collection of Tom Hohman

114

A subtle beauty awaits the hiker in the deep woods of Trail 2.

photo by GJ Greiff

Island, complete with a large swimming pool and a roller coaster named for the natural limestone feature on the site called the Devil's Backbone. Destroyed in the massive Flood of 1937, the Rose Island site a few years later became part of the buffer land surrounding the ammunition plant. A narrow road once led lines of fun seekers in their Model Ts to a suspension bridge, long gone, over Fourteenmile Creek to the Rose Island entrance; a remnant of that road survives today as part of the state park's trail system. A Pratt Truss camelback bridge built in 1912 that once crossed the East Fork of the White River at Portersville on the Daviess-Dubois county line was closed to traffic in 1990. Consisting of two spans totaling over 350 feet, the historic bridge is being moved and installed at the site of the old Rose Island suspension bridge, providing hikers access to the fascinating overgrown ruins of the lost amusement park.[3]

The heavily forested valleys wind amidst rocky outcroppings, and hikers are likely to be startled by the shriek of an osprey seeking a meal of fish in the creek or river. Because the Ohio River into which Fourteenmile Creek flows is controlled with locks and dams, the creek level usually stays artificially high. While the result is that it takes the odd appearance of a linear lake winding through the park, the stream teems with fish for eager anglers. As with most of Indiana's state parks, one is likely to experience nature's wonders best in the autumn or in early spring, when the woods are carpeted with masses of flowers.

NOTES

1. Susan Schramm, "Name That Park," *Indianapolis Star*, 4 February 1994.

2. Pagac, interview with author, 4 March 2003; "New State Parks Would Need Money," *Indianapolis News*, 27 March 1995; author's fieldwork, 30 May 2003.

3. *Ibid.* ; author's interview with Daniel W. Bortner, Director of State Parks and Reservoirs, State of Indiana Department of Natural Resources, 30 June 2008.

FORT HARRISON STATE PARK

(Established 1996)

Master plans for state park acquisition and development had long called for establishing state recreational land near Indianapolis, yet for decades nothing fulfilled the needs of the capital's metropolitan area until the closing of Fort Benjamin Harrison in northeast Marion County provided the opportunity to create a park on the city's doorstep. The property was virtually ready to go, once the park boundaries were determined, because the military installation had established large greenspaces around its borders, especially in the northwest portion and along Fall Creek. There were trails, artificial lakes, and even an eighteen-hole golf course, the first (and only) one in a state park.

After the end of the Spanish-American War at the turn of the twentieth century, the federal government decided to expand the standing army and set up new posts. When the Army closed the Civil War-era United States Arsenal east of downtown, many Hoosiers lobbied to have a new military post built in the vicinity of Indianapolis. Congress authorized the funds in 1903, and Russell B. Harrison urged President Theodore Roosevelt to name the fort for his father, former President (and General) Benjamin Harrison, who had died two years earlier. Fort Harrison opened northeast of Indianapolis in 1906 and became fully operational two years later, serving numerous and fluctuating functions over the next nine decades, including, after World War II, housing the Army Finance Center. After the end of the Cold War in the late twentieth century, the federal government began to cut back and close military installations around the country, and in 1991 the Base Closure and Realignment Commission placed Fort Benjamin Harrison on its list of properties. The fort closed in 1996 amidst considerable wrangling over what was to become of it. About eight hundred acres of mostly built-up area, comprised of a mix of historic buildings (many of which are listed in the National Register of Historic Places), more recent structures, and vacated land for redevelopment, came under the state's Fort Harrison Reuse Authority.[1]

But the bulk of the property, some 1700 acres that includes over three miles of Fall Creek and its tributaries, became Fort Harrison State Park. The park's interpretive center, saddle barns, and office are housed in some of the historic buildings that comprise the Camp Edwin F. Glenn Historic District near the south edge of the property. Camp Glenn had served as a Citizens Military Training Camp (1925-1941), a Civilian Conservation Corps training camp (1933-1941), and, in the

The offices of the park are in a small district listed in the National Register of Historic Places.

photo by GJ Greiff

116

last year of World War II, a Prisoner of War facility. The state park offers a restaurant and conference center adjacent to the golf course, housed in the former Officers' and Civilians' Club. Limited bed-and-breakfast lodging is available in what once were senior officers' living quarters.[2]

For many local citizens, Fort Harrison State Park functions much as a city park. It is common, for example, to see young mothers with strollers and children in tow along the paved multi-use trail. Happily, Fort Harrison's proximity to the city makes it possible for inner-city families to experience a state park simply by hopping on a bus and for urban school children to participate in any number of nature study programs. The park contains one of the largest stands of mature hardwoods in central Indiana, and a hike along its hilly trails can refresh one's spirit with the sound of rippling water or rapping woodpeckers, or the sight of a leaping deer.

The presence of Fort Harrison for ninety years allowed this forest with its lovely trails to mature.   *photo by GJ Greiff*

 NOTES

1. Rex Redifer, "Fort Ben Gave the City a Kinder, Gentler Military," *Indianapolis Star*, 26 May 1991; Rob Schneider, "Day Is Done," *Indianapolis Star*, 29 September 1996; J.R. Ross, "Fort Harrison's Military Life Officially Ends," *South Bend Tribune*, 1 October 1996.

2. "Camp Edwin F. Glenn Historic District," nomination form to National Register of Historic Places (1995), on file at DHPA; Skip Hess, "FORTified," *Indianapolis News*, 4 March 1996.

PROPHETSTOWN STATE PARK
(Established 2004)

Although the need for a state park in the vicinity of Lafayette was identified as early as the 1940s, previous attempts to establish one failed, and indeed, the present park was much delayed by the state's budget difficulties since the first parcels of land were acquired. The site chosen in 1989 was far from impressive at first glance, but the same could be said of many of our state parks when they were but a gleam in the planner's eye. It had almost no trees, as it had been mostly farmland for well over a century; the land is very rich. Not only is the property adjacent to a railroad and Interstate 65, but worse still, a two-lane state highway bisects the site. But the land lies along the history-laden Wabash River and incorporates what is believed to be the site of Prophet's Town, the settlement led by Tenskwatawa, the brother of Shawnee leader Tecumseh, and part of the Tippecanoe battlefield, which had been privately owned and zoned for industrial development. (The state memorial commemorating the Battle of Tippecanoe, fought in 1811 between the forces of United States Army under territorial Governor William Henry Harrison and a confederation of native American tribes united by Tecumseh, lies adjacent to the park, west across the railroad.) In a variety of imaginative ways, park planners have reduced the disruptive impact of the railroad and the highways with buffers of trees and earth mounds, along with strategic placement of use areas, roads, and trails.[1]

Within the boundaries of the state park is a three hundred acre complex called the Museum at Prophetstown. A regional not-for-profit organization, Historic Prophetstown, developed this area separately to interpret the land on several levels: a restored prairie, various exhibits on native Americans of the region, including a reconstructed village, and a 1920s living history farm. History has been a component of the state parks experience since the beginnings under Richard Lieber; the multi-layered museum complex takes this tradition to another level. It is also an experiment in public-private partnership.[2]

This bridge conveys state highway 225 safely through the park property. *photo by GJ Greiff*

Prophetstown State Park offers the delights typical of most state parks—hiking, picnicking, camping—but in an environment that differs from the majority of Indiana's state parks. The intent is for it to remain so. Prophetstown is largely open land, much of it restored prairie and wetlands, alternating with patches of woods—not the stereotypical vision of a state park, but true to its geographic heritage, shaped by glaciers thousands of years ago. A walk through its tall-grass prairies takes one into another world and an earlier time. The beauty of prairie tends to be subtle, except in late summer, when the land shouts with colorful flowers. Standing amidst the waving grasses at this time is a singular and soul-stirring experience.

 NOTES

1. Interview, Pagac, 4 March 2003; see Jeff Swiatek, "Proposed Park Site is Short of Trees, Long on Controversy," *Indianapolis Star*, 10 September 1989

2. Pagac, 4 March 2003; David Griffith, Division of State Parks Planning Section, telephone interview, 15 June 1995; http://www.prophetstown.org/ (Museum at Prophetstown website), 30 May 2003; Interview, Bortner, 20 May 2008.

O'BANNON WOODS STATE PARK
(Dedicated 2004)

It is entirely appropriate that this park was named for the O'Bannon family. When Governor Frank O'Bannon was a state senator in the 1980s, he had nurtured the idea of this tract of land in his beloved Harrison County becoming a state park. The area had been in state hands since the Great Depression, starting out as Harrison State Forest when the Division of Forestry was acquiring numerous new properties to add to its one holding in Clark County. All were on land ill-suited for farming, although this had not prevented settlers in the nineteenth century from trying. By the early twentieth century, the land was played out. Starting in 1929 with Morgan-Monroe State Forest, Indiana established several new state forests over the next few years, including Harrison (later, Harrison-Crawford). The Division immediately erected fire towers on all these new properties, but otherwise there was little development in terms of public use.[1]

But the timing of the land acquisition could not have been better, for in 1933 the New Deal offered numerous work programs for developing public lands. In July 1933 Camp S-54 outside Corydon was established with CCC Company 1556, comprised of veterans, a small number of whom were black. They constructed truck trails and fire lines on the recently acquired state land. When this company moved on, the camp was occupied by Company 517, a segregated company of all African-American young men. They moved to a camp site in the state forest, Camp S-86. During their three year tenure, they constructed trails and roads, a new steel fire tower, a service building, a pumphouse and water supply system, barns, a campground, and shelterhouses, including one overlooking the Ohio River. Carved into its stone floor is the profile of an Indian chief and the inscription "Wyandotte Shelter/1936." The company left Harrison State Forest in 1937 and established a new camp in northern Indiana near South Bend. FERA and WPA workers were employed in the forest as well, chiefly doing roadwork. The state gathered still more land into the state forest, and CCC Company 1592 was established at Camp S-86 in 1941, building more trails and developing picnic groves.[2]

Wyandotte Cave, within Harrison-Crawford State Forest but discontiguous from the rest of the state park, had been used by prehistoric Indians for thousands of years. The cave was named for the local river (but which today is called Blue River) of the same name and was a source of chert, used to fashion stone implements and weapons. It is uncertain exactly when European settlers discovered Wyandotte Cave, but it was likely in the late

Sunset light bathes the bluff overlooking the Ohio River.

photo by GJ Greiff

120

eighteenth century. It was not long after that the cave's saltpeter, used in making gunpowder, was noted and mining operations began. Vats and other artifacts dating to the War of 1812 remain in the cave. Magnesium sulfate, the medicinal Epsom salts, was abundant in the cave and also mined. The earliest commercial tours of Wyandotte Cave, sometimes called the Mammoth Cave of Indiana,were begun in 1850 by the Rothrock family, who had originally purchased the land for a mill site in 1819. The state acquired the property including Wyandotte Cave and nearby Siberts Cave (Little Wyandotte Cave) in 1966. Since 2002, the tours, available seasonally, have been contracted to a private company. Both caves are closed in the winter months to accommodate hibernating bats.[3]

In 1974, in response to a clamor for more recreational areas, the Division of Forestry established the Wyandotte Woods State Recreation Area, a tract of two thousand acres within Harrison-Crawford that encompassed all the recreational facilities constructed by the CCC. The Wyandotte Caves also were included as part of the SRA. The Division developed a group camp at the CCC camp site and built a

swimming pool. After the sudden death in 2003 of Governor Frank O'Bannon, who years before had introduced unsuccessful legislation to designate this land as a state park, it seemed a fitting honor to his memory to revive the idea and name the property for three generations of the O'Bannon family, prominent in public life in Harrison County and statewide. Indiana embraced its twenty-fourth state park in 2004. To help visitors appreciate the land's past, a nineteenth century farmstead site includes a barn, a summer kitchen. and a restored 1850s hay press. And to overcome the Ohio River valley's hot summers, in 2007 a new family aquatic center replaced the long-closed swimming pool.

Shelterhouse and picnic ground built by CCC Company 517.
collection of GJ Greiff

O'Bannon Woods State Park is a wonderful place to wander at any time of year, although summers can swelter here. The woods are lovely in winter, alive with flashes of cardinals amidst the hilly terrain. In spring the same hills are filled with woodland flowers, and in fall the mature trees planted by the CCC blaze with color as one gazes from a cliff onto the winding river below. Something of the spirit of the young men who worked here seems to linger with a gentle sense of pride.

   NOTES

1. "Annual Reports," 1929-1932.

2. Information gleaned from RG35, E115 "Camp Inspection Reports," Boxes 68-69, NA; "Conservation Reports," 1934-1937, passim.

3. http://www.adventureindiana.com/media/wyc/press/back.htm; DNR Division of Forestry, Wyandotte Caves SRA: http://www.in.gov/dnr/11981.htm

FORMER STATE PARKS

Each of the following properties was once a state park. Happily, all remain as public recreational land, some still within the state system, the rest administered by their respective counties.

Muscatatuck State Park

Massive stone steps carry hardy park visitors down to the Muscatatuck River.   *photo by GJ Greiff*

In 1921 the site along the Muscatatuck River known as Vinegar Mills became Indiana's fourth state park; it briefly retained the quaint original name before being changed to that of the river. The citizens of Jennings County raised the funds to purchase a hundred-acre tract between Vernon and North Vernon and donated the land to the state. For decades the rapids, rocky gorges, and tangled forest had drawn artists, nature enthusiasts, and lovers seeking solitude in enchanting surroundings. The mills on the property, as well as a lime kiln, had long crumbled, but a large brick dwelling was soon converted to the Muscatatuck Inn. Over the next fifteen years the acreage doubled, but little of the park was easily accessible until the Works Progress Administration undertook a major development project in 1936. They built the main park road, a parking lot, a large stone-and-timber shelterhouse and a smaller picnic shelter.[1]

The Muscatatuck Inn became widely known for its food and was a popular destination of Sunday drives. The Department constructed some cabins to supplement the few rooms available for overnight accommodations. Muscatatuck

State Park was undeniably beautiful and relatively unspoiled, and indeed offered no small measure of historic interest—the foundations of the mills and a quarry site remain. The park met all of Richard Lieber's criteria, but its size argued against its remaining in the state system. In 1953 the Department of Conservation set up a quail-breeding facility on the property, raising the birds for release by Conservation Clubs throughout the state. The game farm was discontinued in 1962, and the Department converted four of the buildings into a group camp for troubled youths in the summers, as part of the Governor's Youth Rehabilitation Program. Otherwise, Muscatatuck remained little more than a lovely picnic spot with some beautiful—and rigorous—hiking trails. In 1967 the Indiana General Assembly voted to turn the property over to a somewhat reluctant Jennings County, which administers the park today.[2]

Bass Lake State Beach

This tiny property along Indiana's fourth-largest natural lake came into the state park system when establishing beach facilities for families "of small means" was one of the Department's priorities. Nestled amidst the vast marshlands that once dominated most of Indiana's northwest counties, the lake was called Winchetonqua ("Beautiful Waters") by the native Americans who inhabited the area until the 1850s. By the turn of the twentieth century Bass Lake, as it was called by then, was becoming a summer resort for Chicagoans and Hoosiers of the Calumet region. As with so many other of northern Indiana's lakes, private development rapidly encroached upon public access to Bass Lake. To keep the lake open to all the people of Indiana, a group of citizens purchased seven acres along the southwestern shore and presented it to the Department of Conservation in 1931. The state developed a beach using sand from the lake bottom (thereby increasing the property to ten acres) and by 1933 erected a fine bath house pavilion. Throughout the state park system the demand for campsites was great, and in 1957 the little park was expanded to 21 acres, which provided space south across Highway 10 for a modern campground. Such a small parcel might not have remained in the state park system as long as it did, had it not been so near to Tippecanoe River State Park, with which Bass Lake shared administrative staff from 1971 to 2002. In that year, owing to continual budget cuts that began in the late twentieth century, the state transferred the property to Starke County.[3]

Scales Lake State Beach

In 1933 Dr. Travis D. Scales, a banker and former mayor of Boonville, presented the state with a 480-acre tract of stripmined land near town for a public recreational park. The Department of Conservation envisioned the property as a state forest, game preserve, and fish hatchery. Such a large reclamation project was ideally suited for the WPA and its predecessor agencies, whose workers constructed a dam that impounded a lake of over sixty acres, along with fish rearing ponds and accompanying structures. As was typical, the public used the lake and surrounding land—much of which required reforestation—for recreation as well.[4]

123

In response to the growing need for park facilities, especially within easy distance from metropolitan areas, the parcel shifted from the administration of the Division of Forestry to that of State Parks in 1951. With the construction of a new bath house and boat dock, the property officially became Scales Lake State Beach that spring.[5]

Scales Lake in the park of the same name, now administered by Warrick County. *photo by GJ Greiff*

Its size limited the potential of the Scales Lake property, and by the 1960s the Division was turning away from the idea of state beaches in favor of larger recreational areas. The establishment in 1966 of the future Harmonie State Park in Posey County that would serve the Evansville area diminished the significance of Scales Lake still further. In 1969, the General Assembly turned the property over to Warrick County, which administers it today as a county park.[6]

Kankakee State Park

Dedicated in 1952 as the eighteenth state park, the eighteen hundred acres of marshland along the Kankakee River between Lake and Newton counties remained so for only twelve years, when the Division of Fish and Game took over its operation. Today it is LaSalle Fish and Wildlife Area, named for the famed French explorer who was likely the first European to travel the river. Initially Kankakee State Park touted its fine fishing and bird watching opportunities, still the area's primary draw. It offered picnicking and hiking on the south side of the river and housekeeping cabins and boat rental facilities on the north side. Hearkening back to Richard Lieber's ideas of setting aside portions of pre-pioneer Indiana, the park preserved a small (but not pristine) fragment of what once had been the great Kankakee swamp. Its very character prevented it from ever becoming very popular; the average park-goer preferred to avoid the swarms of mosquitoes that infested its bayous, remnants of former bends in the sluggish river.[7]

The Kankakee River at LaSalle Fish and Wildlife Area.
photo by GJ Greiff

124

In 1963, while park attendance throughout the state system averaged 124,563, Kankakee lured only 11,678 visitors. With the acquisition of over twelve hundred acres known as the "Baker Ranch" south of the river, the Department felt that a more suitable use of the land would be to operate it as a fish and game area, which allowed hunting as well as fishing.[8] The Department transferred the property to the Division of Fish and Game (today, Fish and Wildlife) in 1964.

Richard Lieber State Park

The property that became Indiana's nineteenth state park seemed not entirely an appropriate memorial to the founder who wrote so passionately of pristine nature. Under the auspices of the Flood Control Act of 1938, the Army Corps of Engineers began to acquire land along the Putnam-Owen county line near Cloverdale in 1947, despite considerable protest by local farm owners. Actual construction of a reservoir, named Cagles Mill Lake, started the following year and was finally completed in 1953.[9] The Army in 1952 transferred the administration of the property to the Department of Conservation, which immediately effected a ten-year development plan that included facilities for fishing, boating,

Eagles and hawks are a frequent and stirring sight above Cataract Lake. *photo by GJ Greiff*

and swimming. At first the emerging recreational area was called Cagles Mill State Forest. The Division of Forestry transferred the property to the Division of State Parks, Lands and Waters in 1956, and by executive order the name became Cataract Lake State Recreation Area. In 1958, 561 acres touching the northeast side of the reservoir became Richard Lieber State Park to preserve the memory of the system's first director.[10] Stretching reality a bit, Governor Harold Handley said Lieber's namesake park "constitutes the ultimate in state park completeness—vast acreages of natural woods, spacious retreats for camping and picnicking . . . facilities for boating and swimming, all of it within easy distance of our large metropolitan centers."[11] The lake itself and the surrounding land, comprising over 7500 acres, was leased to the Department of Conservation by the Army.

In 1966 Agnes Stuckey, owner of the Cataract Falls area on Mill Creek near to where it enters the reservoir on the south, donated the Upper Falls and thirty-five acres to the recently reorganized Department of Natural Resources. Geographic confusion must have run rampant, what with Lieber State Park, Owen-Putnam State Forest, and what was still officially called the Cagles Mill Flood Control Reservoir, publicly known as Cataract Lake. Until 1995 the Division of Reservoir Management that was established in 1968 administered the entire property of over eight thousand acres, still under a lease arrangement with the

125

Army Corps of Engineers. Cagles Mill Lake permits motorboating, but its purpose remains flood control first, recreation second. Ironically, with the sudden merging of the divisions of State Parks and Reservoir Management effected in 1996, the property is once again under the same administration as state parks, although the differences in management and usage policies remain. The former state park is now Lieber State Recreation Area, offering the typical pursuits of fishing, swimming, and camping.[12] For all practical purposes, the public notes little difference.

Raccoon Lake State Recreation Area

Picnic shelter built in the 1960s overlooking the lake.

photo by GJ Greiff

In 1961 Governor Handley dedicated what was called Indiana's twenty-first state park on the shores of a new 2100-acre lake formed by impounding Raccoon Creek in eastern Parke County. Mansfield Reservoir, a project of the Army Corps of Engineers, was the state's second flood control reservoir. In an arrangement similar to that of Cataract Lake, the Army Engineers gave over the operation of all recreational facilities to the Department of Conservation's Division of State Parks. Located on a broad peninsula of approximately 600 acres jutting southward into the lake, the park quickly became a popular destination for the ever growing number of campers that emerged in the decades following World War II. As the Corps of Engineers continued to build more reservoirs in Indiana, administration of adjacent recreational lands became more complicated, particularly since restrictions imposed on water use in state parks did not apply to the reservoirs. In 1968 the Natural Resources Commission established the Division of Reservoir Management within the Department of Natural Resources specifically to handle recreation on the large flood control reservoirs created in the 1960s, such as Monroe and Salamonie. In 1979 Raccoon Lake SRA on Cecil M. Hardin (formerly Mansfield) Reservoir was transferred to this division from the Division of State Parks, along with the former Lieber State Park.[13] Although the differences in management and usage policy remain, the reservoir properties are once again under the same administration with state parks, for in 1996, the divisions of State Parks and Reservoir Management merged.

 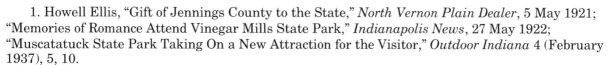

1. Howell Ellis, "Gift of Jennings County to the State," *North Vernon Plain Dealer*, 5 May 1921; "Memories of Romance Attend Vinegar Mills State Park," *Indianapolis News*, 27 May 1922; "Muscatatuck State Park Taking On a New Attraction for the Visitor," *Outdoor Indiana* 4 (February 1937), 5, 10.

2. Myrtie Barker, "What Better Place to Picnic Than on the Banks of the Muscatatuck?" *Indianapolis News*, 2 May 1956; "Conservation Reports," 1962, 5, 27; 1963, 8; "Muscatatuck Park to Be Turned Over to County If Bill Passes," *North Vernon Sun*, 4 February 1967; "Muscatatuck State Park Faces Closing," *Indianapolis Star*, 2 March 1968; "DNR Report," 1968, 47; Hasenstab, telephone interview, 15 May 1995.

3. See "Conservation Reports," 1932, 380, 1958, 32; "DNR Report," 1972, 77; "Bass Lake Beach Popular Outing Place for Swimmers During Vacation Months," *Outdoor Indiana* 6 (December 1939), 15; *Bass Lake State Beach* trail map, published by DNR, 1988.

4. "Gift of 477 Acres in Warrick County for State Park," *Indianapolis Star*, 11 December 1933; RG79, E44 "Records Concerning WPA Projects," Box 4, NA; "Conservation Report," 1935, 437, 442; "Relief Changed from Dole to Work," *Indianapolis Star*, 25 January 1936; "Fish Hatchery and Lake Are Nearing Completion at Scales Lake Forest," *Outdoor Indiana* 3 (March 1936), 30-31; "Lands Given to Public Use Developed Under WPA Program," *Recovery in Indiana* (June 1936), 3.

5. "Conservation Report," 1951, 7, 10-11.

6. "DNR Report," 1969, 42.

7. "Conservation Reports," 1947, 673, 713; 1954, 30.

8. See Thomas B. March, "Kankakee State Park Becomes LaSalle State Fish and Game Area," *Outdoor Indiana* 30 (March 1964), 16-19.

9. "Building of Cagles Mill Dam Started," *Indianapolis News*, 2 July 1948; "80 Landowners Resent Deals at Cagles Mill," *Indianapolis Times*, 12 December 1948; "Cagles Mill: Newest Conservation Acquisition," *Outdoor Indiana* 16 (October 1949), 6-7; "Dedication of Cagles Mill Set for June 18," *Outdoor Indiana* 19 (June 1952), 19.

10. "Cagle Mill Area Transferred to State in Ceremonies June 19," *Outdoor Indiana* 19 (August 1952), 14; "Conservation Report," 1955, 3; "19th State Park," *Indianapolis News*, 12 July 1958; "Dedication Program for Richard Lieber State Park," July 12, 1958.

11. Handley quoted in "Indiana Dedicates Newest Park," *Indianapolis Star*, 13 July 1958.

12. "Master Plan for Cataract Falls Unit of Richard Lieber State Park," Indiana Department of Natural Resources Engineering Division (February 1969).

13. Henry C. Prange, "The new Mansfield Reservoir and Raccoon Lake State Recreation Area," *Outdoor Indiana* 28 (August 1961), 19-23; "Governor Dedicates State's 21st Park," *Indianapolis Star*, 10 September 1961; Joseph R. Keel, "Raccoon Lake Popular With Hoosier Campers," *Indianapolis Star*, 11 August 1963; Favinger, "Environmental Era," 29-30.

SELECTED BIBLIOGRAPHY

PRIMARY SOURCES

Manuscript Collections

National Archives, Washington, D.C.
. Record Group 35, Records of the Civilian Conservation Corps
. Record Group 69, Records of the Works Progress Administration
. Record Group 79, Records of the National Park Service

Commission on Public Records (State Archives), Indianapolis
. Administrative Files of the Indiana Department of Conservation
. Governors Files, Paul V. McNutt Papers
. Florence Grady Ernsting Secretarial Papers

Franklin D. Roosevelt Presidential Library, Hyde Park, New York
. Wayne Coy Papers
. Harry O. Hopkins Papers
. Official Files

Manuscripts Department, Lilly Library, Indiana University, Bloomington
. Paul V. Brown Manuscripts
. John K. Jennings Manuscripts
. Richard Lieber Manuscripts
. Indiana WPA Manuscripts

Indiana Division, Indiana State Library, Indianapolis
. Clipping Files, CCC
. Clipping Files, Indiana State Parks
. Clipping Files, WPA

Library, Division of State Parks, Indianapolis

Archival Files, individual Indiana state park offices

Newspapers and Periodicals

Indianapolis News, 1915-1995.

Indianapolis Star, 1915-2008.

Indianapolis Times, 1933-1942.

Outdoor Indiana, 1934-1990.

Pulaski County Democrat (Winamac), 1934-1940.

Recreation, 1935-1937.

Government Documents

"Annual Reports of Department of Conservation," *Yearbook of the State of Indiana* [1916-1950], Indianapolis, 1917-1951.

Annual Reports of the Indiana Department of Conservation. Indianapolis, 1951-1965.

Annual Reports of the Indiana Department of Geology and Natural Resources. Indianapolis, 1900-1916.

Annual Reports of the Indiana Department of Natural Resources. Indianapolis, 1965-1991.

Annual Reports of the State Board of Forestry. Indianapolis: Wm. B. Burford, 1901-1920.

The CCC and Its Contribution to a Nation-Wide State Park Recreational Program. Washington: United States Department of the Interior, 1937.

Governor's Commission on Unemployment Relief. *Recovery in Indiana*. Indianapolis, 1934-1936.

National Park Service, United States Department of Interior. *Park and Recreation Structures*. 3 volumes. Washington, D.C.: U.S. Government Printing Office, 1938.

National Park Service, United States Department of Interior. *Yearbook: Park and Recreation Progress*. 4 editions. Washington, D.C.: U.S. Government Printing Office, 1938-1942.

Report on Progress of WPA Program. 4 volumes. Washington, D.C.: U.S. Government Printing Office, 1939-1942.

"State Parks Manual." Indianapolis: Indiana Department of Public Works, 1937.

Other Printed Primary Material

Dearborn, Ned H. *Once in a Lifetime: A Guide to the CCC Camp*. Chicago: Charles E. Merrill Company, 1936.

Evison, Herbert, ed. *A State Park Anthology*. Washington, D.C.: National Conference on State Parks, 1930.

Hopkins, Harry. *Spending to Save: The Complete Story of Relief*. New York: W.W. Norton, 1936.

Howard, Donald S. *The WPA and Federal Relief Policy*. New York: Russell Sage Foundation, 1943.

Hoyt, Ray. *"We Can Take It": A Short Story of the C.C.C.* New York: American Book Company, 1935.

Lieber, Richard. *America's Natural Wealth: A Story of the Use and Abuse of Our Resources*. New York: Harper and Brothers, 1942.

Lindley, Betty and Ernest K. Lindley. *A New Deal for Youth: The Story of the National Youth Administration*. New York: Viking Press, 1938.

McEntee, James J. *Now They Are Men: The Story of the CCC*. Washington, D.C.: National Home Library Foundation, 1940.

Nelson, Beatrice Ward. *State Recreation: Parks, Forests and Game Preserves*. Washington, D.C.: National Conference on State Parks, 1928.

Nixon, Edgar B., comp. and ed. *Franklin D. Roosevelt and Conservation, 1911-1945*. 2 volumes. Hyde Park: Franklin D. Roosevelt Library, 1957.

Pinchot, Gifford. *Breaking New Ground*. New York: Harcourt, Brace and Company, 1947.

Rosenman, Samuel I., ed. *The Court Disapproves*. Volume 4 of *The Public Papers and Addresses of Franklin D. Roosevelt*. New York: Random House, 1938.

_____.*The Year of Crisis, 1933*. Volume 2 of *The Public Papers and Addresses of Franklin D. Roosevelt*. New York: Random House, 1938.

Torrey, Raymond H. *State Parks and Recreational Uses of State Forests in the United States*. Washington, D.C.: National Conference on State Parks, 1926.

Works Projects Administration. . *Indiana: A Guide to the Hoosier State*. New York: Oxford University Press, 1941.

Articles

Frazier, Corrine Reid. "Why Pay the Fiddler?" *The Parents' Magazine* (February 1937), 20-21, 71-74.

Stevens, James. "Indiana's Magnificent McNutt," *American Mercury* (August 1937), 430-437.

Interviews

Bortner, Daniel W., Director of State Parks and Reservoirs, State of Indiana Department of Natural Resources. Interviews by author, 20 May and 30 June 2008. Notes in posession of author.

Foltz, Donald, former Director, Indiana Department of Conservation. Interview by author, 9 April 1994, Centenary, Indiana. Transcript on file at Indiana Historical Society [hereafter IHS].

Hasenstab, Louis, former Director of Recreation, Indiana Division of State Parks. Interviews by author, 18 February and 2 March 1993, Indianapolis. Transcripts on file at IHS.

Heaton, Mac [Malcolm], former Art Director, Indiana Department of Conservation. Interview by author, 26 April 1993, Carmel, Indiana. Transcript on file at IHS.

Nicholson, Roberta West, former WPA administrator. Interview by author, 16 February 1982, Brown County, Indiana. Tape and transcript in possession of author.

Pagac, Gerald, Director, Indiana Division of State Parks. Interviews by author, 3 February 1993, Indianapolis, Indiana. Transcript on file at IHS. 4 March 2003, Indianapolis, Indiana. Tape recording in possession of author.

Ping, Walter, CCC veteran (Clifty Falls State Park). Interview by author, 19 December 1990, Indianapolis. Tape recording in possession of author.

Ralston, Patrick, and Jack [John R.] Costello, Director and Deputy Director, respectively, Indiana Department of Natural Resources. Joint interview by author, 26 January 1993, Indianapolis, Indiana. Transcript on file at IHS.

Skinner, Gerald, former WPA worker (Lawrence County). Interview by author, 30 December 1981, Oolitic, Indiana. Tape recording in possession of author.

Woodcock, Roger, CCC veteran (Pokagon State Park). Interview by author, 3 November 1990, Corunna, Indiana. Tape and transcript in possession of author.

SECONDARY SOURCES

Books

Armstrong, Ellis L., ed. *History of Public Works in the United States, 1776-1976*. Chicago: American Public Works Association, 1976.

Butler, Ovid, ed. *American Conservation in Picture and in Story*. Washington, D.C.: American Forestry Association, 1935.

Carlson, Reynold E. *et al. Recreation in American Life*. Belmont, Calif.: Wadsworth Publishing Company, 1963.

Conard, Rebecca. *Places of Quiet Beauty: Parks, Preserves, and Environmentalism*. Iowa City: University of Iowa Press, 1997.

Conkin, Paul K. *The New Deal*. New York: Thomas Y. Crowell Company, 1967.

Cox, Thomas R. *The Park Builders: A Comparative History of State Parks in the Pacific Northwest*. Seattle: University of Washington Press, 1988.

Cutler, Phoebe. *The Public Landscape of the New Deal*. New Haven: Yale University Press, 1985.

Degler, Carl N., ed. *The New Deal*. Chicago: Quadrangle Books, 1970.

Doell, Charles E., and Gerald B. Fitzgerald. *A Brief History of Parks and Recreation in the United States*. Chicago: Athletic Institute, 1954.

Dulles, Foster Rhea. *America Learns to Play: A History of Popular Recreation, 1607-1940.* Gloucester, Mass.: Peter Smith, 1959.

Dunlap, Thomas R. *Saving America's Wildlife.* Princeton: Princeton University Press, 1988.

Flader, Susan L. *Exploring Missouri's Legacy: State Parks and Historic Sites.* Columbia: University of Missouri Press, 1992.

_____, *Thinking Like a Mountain: Aldo Leopold and the Evolution of An Ecological Attitude Toward Deer, Wolves, and Forests.* Columbia: University of Missouri Press, 1974.

Fox, Stephen. *John Muir and His Legacy: The American Conservation Movement.* Boston: Little, Brown and Company, 1981.

Freidel, Frank. *Franklin D. Roosevelt: Launching the New Deal.* Boston: Little, Brown and Company, 1973.

_____, ed. *The New Deal and the American People.* Englewood Cliffs, N.J.: Prentice-Hall, 1964.

Hays, Samuel P. *Conservation and the Gospel of Efficiency: The Progressive Conservation Movement, 1890-1920.* Cambridge: Harvard University Press, 1959.

Huthmacher, J. Joseph. *Trial by War and Depression, 1917-1941.* Boston: Allyn and Bacon, 1973.

Kieley, James F. *A Brief History of the National Park Service.* Washington, D.C.: U.S. Department of the Interior, 1940.

Korn, Claire V. *Michigan State Parks: Yesterday Through Tomorrow.* East Lansing: Michigan State University Press, 1989.

Lacy, Leslie Alexander. *The Soil Soldiers: The Civilian Conservation Corps in the Great Depression.* Radnor, Pa.: Chilton Book Company, 1976.

Leuchtenberg, William. *Franklin D. Roosevelt and the New Deal.* New York: Harper & Row, 1963.

McCall, Joseph R., and Virginia N. McCall. *Outdoor Recreation: Forest Park, and Wilderness.* Beverly Hills: Benziger, Bruce and Glencoe, 1977.

McClelland, Linda Flint. *Presenting Nature: The Historic Landscape Design of the National Park Service, 1916 to 1942.* Washington, D.C.: National Park Service, 1993.

McGeary, M. Nelson. *Gifford Pinchot: Forester-Politician.* Princeton: Princeton University Press, 1960.

Mackintosh, Barry. *The National Parks: Shaping the System.* Washington, D.C.: National Park Service, 1988.

Madison, James H. *Indiana Through Tradition and Change: A History of the Hoosier State and Its People, 1920-1945.* Indianapolis: Indiana Historical Society, 1982.

Meine, Curt. *Aldo Leopold, His Life and Work.* Madison: University of Wisconsin Press, 1988.

Merrill, Perry H. *Roosevelt's Forest Army: A History of the Civilian Conservation Corps, 1933-1942.* Montpelier: Merrill, 1981.

Meyer, Roy W. *Everyone's Country Estate: A History of Minnesota's State Parks.* St. Paul: Minnesota Historical Society Press, 1991.

Nash, Roderick Frazier. *American Environmentalism: Readings in Conservation History.* New York: McGraw-Hill, 1990.

_____. *Wilderness and the American Mind.* New Haven: Yale University Press, 1967.

Newton, Norman T. *Design on the Land: The Development of Landscape Architecture.* Cambridge: Belknap Press, 1971.

Owen, A.L. Riesch. *Conservation Under FDR.* New York: Praeger Books, 1983.

Paige, John C. *The Civilian Conservation Corps and the National Park Service, 1933-1942: An Administrative History.* Washington: U.S. Government Printing Office, 1985.

Phillips, Clifton J. *Indiana in Transition: The Emergence of an Industrial Commonwealth, 1880-1920.* Indianapolis: Indiana Historical Bureau and Indiana Historical Society, 1968.

Rainwater, Clarence Elmer. *The Play Movement in the United States: A Study of Community Recreation.* Chicago: University of Chicago Press, 1921.

Runte, Alfred. *National Parks: The American Experience.* Lincoln: University of Nebraska Press, 1979.

Salmond, John A. *The Civilian Conservation Corps, 1933-1942: A New Deal Case Study.* Durham: Duke University Press, 1967.

Scarpino, Philip V. *Great River: An Environmental History of the Upper Mississippi, 1890-1950.* Columbia: University of Missouri Press, 1985.

Schlesinger, Arthur M., Jr. *The Coming of the New Deal.* Volume II of *The Age of Roosevelt.* Boston: Houghton Mifflin Company, 1959.

_____.*The Politics of Upheaval.* Volume III of *The Age of Roosevelt.* Boston: Houghton Mifflin Company, 1960.

Schmitt, Peter J. *Back to Nature: The Arcadian Myth in Urban America.* New York: Oxford University Press, 1969.

Sitkoff, Harvard, ed. *Fifty Years Later: The New Deal Evaluated.* New York: Alfred A. Knopf, 1985.

Terkel, Studs. *Hard Times: An Oral History of the Great Depression.* New York: Pantheon Books, 1970.

Utley, Robert M., and Barry Mackintosh. *The Department of Everything Else: Highlights of Interior History.* Washington, D.C.: Department of Interior, 1989.

Williams, Michael. *Americans and Their Forests: A Historical Geography.* Cambridge: Cambridge University Press, 1989.

Wirth, Conrad L. *Parks, Politics, and the People.* Norman: University of Oklahoma Press, 1980.

Worster, Donald. *Nature's Economy: A History of Ecological Ideas.* Cambridge: Cambridge University Press, 1985.

Zinn, Howard, ed. *New Deal Thought.* New York: Bobbs-Merrill Company, 1966.

Articles

Ahlgren, Carol. "The Civilian Conservation Corps and Wisconsin State Park Development." *Wisconsin Magazine of History* (Spring 1988), 184-216.

Conard, Rebecca. "Hot Kitchens in Places of Quiet Beauty: Iowa State Parks and the Transformation of Conservation Goals." *The Annals of Iowa* 51 (Summer 1992) 441-479.

Donahue, Bernard. "Politics and Federal-State Programs for the Unemployed: The Case of the Indiana WPA." *Humboldt Journal of Social Relations* 6 (Spring-Summer 1979), 159-183.

Greiff, Glory-June. "Roads, Rocks, and Recreation: The Legacy of the WPA in Indiana." *Traces* 3 (Summer 1991), 40-47.

Hendrickson, Kenneth E., Jr. "Relief for Youth: The Civilian Conservation Corps and the National Youth Administration in North Dakota." *North Dakota History Journal of the Northern Plains* 48 (Fall 1981), 17-27.

Muller, Herman J. "The Civilian Conservation Corps, 1933-1942." *Historical Bulletin* 28 (March 1950), 55-60.

Runte, Alfred. "Preservation Heritage: The Origins of the Park Idea in the United States." *Lectures 1983: Perceptions of the Landscape and Its Preservation.* Indianapolis: Indiana Historical Society, 1984, 53-75.

Silver, David M., ed. "Richard Lieber and Indiana's Forest Heritage." *Indiana Magazine of History* 65 (March 1971), 45-55.

Weir, L.H. "Historical Background of the Recreation Movement in America." *Parks and Recreation* 29 (July-August 1946), 238-243.

Unpublished Works

Eagelman, James P. "Washington Township: The Brown County Forest Story from 1780 to 1980." Master's thesis, Depauw University, 1980.

Frederick, Robert Allen. "Colonel Richard Lieber, Conservationist and Park Builder: The Indiana Years." Ph.D. dissertation, Indiana University, 1960.

Greiff, Glory-June. "New Deal Resources in Indiana State Parks." Discrete study for the Indiana Historic Sites and Structures Inventory, Indiana Division of Historic Preservation and Archaeology, 1991.

_____. "New Deal Resources on Indiana State Lands." Discrete field study of state forests, fish and wildlife areas, fish hatcheries, and the like for the Indiana Historic Sites and Structures Inventory, Indiana Division of Historic Preservation and Archaeology, 1996.

_____. "New Deal Work Projects in Indiana State Parks." Historic context for Indiana Division of Historic Preservation and Archaeology, 1991.

_____. "Parks for the People: New Deal Work Projects in Indiana State Parks." Master's thesis, Indiana University, 1992.

Hasenstab, Louis. "The Conservation Awakening." Draft manuscript dated 28 September 1990, on file at Indiana Division of State Parks.

Murphy, William Daniel. "A History of State Parks and Recreation Areas in Nebraska." Ph.D. dissertation, Indiana University, 1975.

Pruitt, Straussa V. "Indiana State Parks--Their Educational Contributions." Master's thesis, Indiana State Teachers College, 1936.

Sherraden, Michael W. "The Civilian Conservation Corps: The Effectiveness of the Camps." Ph.D. dissertation, University of Michigan, 1979.

INDEX

APPENDIX

State Park Directors

Richard Lieber	1916-1933	Director of Conservation
Charles G. Sauers	1919-1929	Assistant to Director
Paul V. Brown	1929-1933	Assistant to Director
Myron Rees	1933-1938	Director of State Parks and Lands and Waters
Charles A. DeTurk	1939-1945	Director of State Parks and Lands and Waters
Robert F. Wirsching	1946-1947	Director of State Parks, Lands and Waters
Kenneth R. Cougill	1947-1964	Director of State Parks, Lands and Waters
Robert Starrett	1964-1966	Director of State Parks
Joseph A. Blatt	1966-1970	Director of State Parks
G.T. Donceel	1970-1971	Acting Director of State Parks
David Herbst	1971-1977	Director of State Parks
William C. Walters	1977-1989	Director of State Parks
Gerald J. Pagac	1989-2005	Director of State Parks and Reservoirs
Daniel W. Bortner	2005-	Director of State Parks and Reservoirs

This project received federal financial assistance for the identification and protection of historic properties. Under Title VI of the Civil Rights Act of 1964, Section 504 of the Rehabilitation Act of 1973, and the Age of Discrimination Act of 1975, the U.S. Department of the Interior prohibits discrimination on the basis of race, color, national origin, disability, or age in its federally assisted programs. If you believe you have been discriminated against in any program, activity, or facility as described above, or if you desire further information, please write to: Director, Office of Equal Opportunity, National Park Service, 1849 C Street NW, Washington, D.C. 20240.